Truth in the
Arctic

Truth in the Arctic

Jack Turner

David Luckman

CF4•K

10 9 8 7 6 5 4 3 2 1

Copyright © 2022 David Luckman
Paperback ISBN: 978-1-5271-0792-2
Ebook ISBN: 978-1-5271-0870-7

Published by Christian Focus Publications,
Geanies House, Fearn, Tain, Ross-shire,
IV20 1TW, Scotland, U.K.
www.christianfocus.com;
email: info@christianfocus.com

Cover design by Jeff Anderson
Cover illustration by Jeff Anderson
Printed and bound by Nørhaven, Denmark

Contents

24th September 1947 7

Fun and Adventure 19

A Change of Direction 27

Preparation for Service 35

Journey to the Arctic.................................... 45

A Missionary's Life 53

On the Trail 61

Returning Home 69

A New Mission Station 81

Corn Flakes, All Bran and Puffed Rice 91

Going on a Bear Hunt 99

Here comes the Bride................................... 109

Operation Canon 119

Author Information 130

Jack Turner Timeline 131

Thinking Further Topics 133

Members of the Operation Canon Rescue Team 138

Medical Specialists at Winnipeg General Hospital 139

Map 140

24th September 1947

Rebecca and Elizabeth wrapped up well before venturing out into the freezing cold air, swinging their buckets. The water in the house was running low and they needed to get some more from outside. The sharp wind blew so hard it hurt their hands and faces. Nevertheless, they had a job to do and they were happy to do it. They were local Inuit girls who loved to help the Turner family. Rebecca had known the Turners all her life and was now assisting them on a daily basis. Elizabeth was from the local village of Moffet Inlet. This particular day, Mrs Turner asked them to go out into the snow, break up some ice and bring it inside the house to be thawed for fresh drinking water.

The Arctic winter was approaching, and the girls struggled in the harsh snowy conditions of that late September morning to fill their buckets with ice. However, Rebecca and Elizabeth would not be defeated by the wintry conditions. When they had filled their containers to the brim, they shuffled through the snow and into the enclosure around the house. The young helpers climbed slowly and carefully up the few steps onto the porch. Their buckets were heavy when full of ice. Back inside, they emptied their load into a large basin by the stove to melt. Elizabeth was smaller and younger than Rebecca who was fourteen and towered above her, but she helped as best she could.

Canon John Turner was upstairs in the loft, thinking how he could turn it into a bedroom. His wife Joan was expecting their third child in a few months and the extra space would be welcomed. They had two daughters. June was the eldest child, born on 4th June 1945, hence her name. Grace arrived the following year, 21st September 1946.

The four of them lived in a small home that was built close to the bay of Moffet Inlet on Baffin Island, in the most northerly part of Canada called the Arctic. The little wooden structure had survived a decade of extreme Arctic weather. Jack, as he was known, recalled the December day back in 1937 when he started to build it with the help of some of the local Inuit men. He remembered how the extremely bleak conditions made the task very hard. The temperature that day had dropped to minus 41 degrees Celsius and he couldn't hold on to his tools very well. Later that evening, when his hands had warmed up, he wrote in his diary that the building experience was 'cold on hands!' The memory made Jack chuckle, as he wrapped the warm fingers of his right hand around the wooden handle of the hammer. It was easier to make changes inside the house, especially as the weather outside was so brisk and dreary.

Not all of Jack's friends understood why he would leave his home in England and spend the rest of his life in the freezing climate of Baffin Land as a missionary. As far as they were concerned, Jack had everything going for him. He was very sporty at school, captaining the cricket and football teams. He was musical at college, and he was always fun to be with. Jack had a constant cheerful disposition which made him likeable to almost everyone he met. He could do anything he wanted, his friends thought. What would take him to the frozen wastelands of the Arctic? Surely Jack knew that it was one of the most inhospitable and dangerous parts of the world to live in, because of the desolate landscape and extremely cold weather?

It was a simple matter of love that would take Jack there. He loved the Lord Jesus with all his heart, and he wanted to serve the Lord Jesus with all his life. As a young Christian man, he had been challenged to serve Jesus Christ in the Arctic: how would the Inuit people of that frosty wasteland know that their greatest need is to have their sins forgiven by God, if there was no one willing to go and tell them?

The challenge pierced Jack's heart, like an arrow loosed hard and fast at a target. He decided that he would do it. He would go to the Inuit to tell them of the Master's love.

It wouldn't be easy to reach the Arctic's native population. The Arctic was rugged and treacherous. Freezing temperatures, snowy blizzards and icy winds cut any exposed area of flesh like a sharp knife. They would all come together to make the gospel mission to the Inuit perilous. The winter months were long and dark. Jack was made aware that missionaries in the Arctic experienced long periods of isolation cut off from the world. Letters from friends and family in England only arrived at the shores of Baffin Land once a year by ship. The valiant servant of Christ would need determination and a cheerful outlook to survive this special task.

In his eighteen years as a missionary in the Arctic, Jack travelled many of the unmapped districts of the frozen wilderness to bring the gospel of Jesus Christ to the people. He knew only too well what it meant to face the harsh bite of the Arctic cold in search of God's people. Yet he would do it gladly, for the word of God and the testimony of Jesus Christ (Revelation 1:9).

As the girls collected ice, Jack could hear them talking kindly to his dogs that were also braving the cold outside. He had sixteen husky dogs that he used for pulling his sledge from one camp to another. Jack's concern was that he hadn't enough food stored up for them to survive the winter. Like the Inuit men in Moffet Inlet, Jack would hunt for dog food. Polar bear, seal, caribou, fish from the frozen waters – all good food for human and dog consumption.

As the two young girls were walking back to the house laden with ice, they spotted a seal in the water near the shore of the bay. Through the whistling wind in the attic, Jack could faintly hear Rebecca shouting, "Canon Jack, there is a seal in the bay!"

Jack quickly dropped his hammer and ran down the stairs to fetch his rifle. He couldn't miss this opportunity to hunt for food for the dogs. Hastily he pulled on his seal skinned boots and coat made of caribou fur. He saw Joan standing by the stove, looking at him quizzically.

'Seal in the bay!' he remarked excitedly, as he pecked her on the cheek. He then dashed out the door on to the veranda with his rifle in his hands.

'It's over there, Canon Jack!' yelled Elizabeth pointing to the far corner of the inlet. Jack looked and could barely see the grey head of the seal poking out of the icy water near the shore. It was time to hunt. His dogs depended on him to provide enough food for them to survive the winter.

Jack bounded down the three steps into the enclosure around the house, and through the gate onto the ragged surface of the bay. He strode quickly past the girls and headed in the direction of the seal. After a moment the girls could hear the cracking noise of the gun, as Jack took aim and fired at his prey. He missed. The sound startled the seal who made its escape by diving under the water's surface. Jack knew that his opportunity was gone. He turned on his heels and made his way back to the house.

He caught up with Elizabeth at the gate to the enclosure. Elizabeth's bucket was heavy, and Jack could see that she was struggling with it. He was a caring and thoughtful person by nature. Looking at his young assistant, he said, 'Elizabeth, let me help you with your bucket.' Elizabeth smiled at him, as Jack slipped his rifle under his left arm and reached for the bucket. Together they walked through the enclosure and up the steps onto the porch. The wind and snow continued to swirl around their heads. As they reached the top step, Jack's rifle slipped under his arm. The trigger was released, and a bullet shot out of the rifle, through Jack's top lip and stopped at the base of his skull. He fell backwards down the steps into the snow, hitting his lower back on the corner of the top platform. The snow around his mouth turned dark red as blood poured from the wound. Jack lay there, motionless. His breathing was laboured, but at least he was still alive. He needed help, and fast.

It came from the Tongalok family who were living close by. They were native people who came to know and love the Lord Jesus through Jack's Christian witness to them. Over the years Jack helped the Tongaloks to follow Christ faithfully, and they loved Jack for his kindness and care of them.

Joan wasn't aware that anything had happened to her husband until Mrs Tongalok ran into the house and shouted something incomprehensible to her. From the way that her friend was behaving, Joan knew that something bad had happened. She darted to the door. Her gaze fell to her husband lying at the bottom of the steps, unconscious on the ground. She needed to get him out of the cold and inside. Joan moved quickly up the stairs to the bedroom. She threw blankets and a mattress down the stairs and prepared a bed for Jack on the floor of his little study, next to the sparsely furnished sitting room.

Mrs Turner was expecting another baby in a few months and she knew that it would be hard for her to lift Jack up the steps and into the home. She was grateful to have the help of David Tongalok, who bore much of Jack's weight as they carried him to the makeshift bed in his study. They gently lowered Jack on to the mattress. Joan covered him with blankets to keep him warm. Once Jack was settled, it was time to pray. David took his family into the kitchen and led them in prayer. As they knelt, they earnestly asked God to help their wounded friend and mentor. At the same time, Joan kneeled by Jack's bed. She affectionately held his hand and prayed quietly with her injured husband. Joan knew that her training as a nurse would be called upon in her husband's hour of need. She also knew that someone had to go for help. The nearest radio was seventy miles away in Arctic Bay and the weather was still too rough to travel. David Tongalok assured Joan that he would go for help once the weather calmed.

By seven o'clock that evening of the 24th September 1947, David started his journey to Arctic Bay. He had never handled 'Ebenezer' (Jack's boat) before, but he was willing to do whatever he could to help his dearly loved friends.

David made the hazardous journey along the west coast of Baffin Island, from Moffet Inlet to Arctic Bay. As he moved closer to the shore, he heard the strange sound of husky dogs barking in reaction to the whine of old Ebenezer's engine. Through the dimness he could see a handful of dark wooden huts dotted around the shoreline. Soft light shone through the windows of the community, willing David safely to shore.

Behind the scattered homes lay the majestic cliffs of the bay that gave the small hamlet shelter from the land's icy gusts. The sea at the mouth of the cove was frozen solid. It was going to be difficult for the decrepit boat to get close to the trading post. The ice cracked and moaned as it felt the pressure of the water beneath the hull of the vessel slowly edging forward to its goal.

David thought of Canon Jack Turner. He remembered the wounded Arctic missionary lying unconscious on a mattress on the floor of the little study in the mission house. He remembered Mrs Turner kneeling at her husband's side, holding his hand and wiping his brow. She prayed to the Lord that he would watch over her husband, to whom she was completely devoted. As David entered the bay, he prayed that he was not too late to help the friend whom he had come to love and deeply respect.

When the boat could travel no further, David leapt out onto the ice and started for the door of the Hudson's Bay Company trading post. His destination was one of a number of isolated trading stations dotted around the coastline of Baffin Island.

The Hudson's Bay Company made its fortune trading furs and things for the home. Each post was staffed by the only other 'white' men in the land, apart from the missionaries. The locals would travel from the surrounding villages and trade any seal or deer furs from successful hunting trips. Each trading post had a radio station so that the staff could keep in touch with the rest of the Dominion of Canada. This was exactly why David slipped and slided his way to the Company's door. He knew that he could get the help he needed there.

Pounding on the entrance, he called out, 'Is there anyone inside? Open up! I need help!' He kept knocking hard on the door. He kept calling out for help, so much so that he couldn't hear the footsteps of Mr Cormack scurrying across the room in response to David's distress.

'Whatever is the matter?!' exclaimed the trading master as he opened the door briskly.

David quickly moved inside the room, stamping his feet with each step. The snow fell off his boots and quickly melted on the timber floor of the warm cabin. As he took down his thick fur hood, his dark eyes locked on to the gaze of Mr Cormack, the post manager. David began to tell the terrible account of what had taken place seventy miles south at Moffet Inlet. He needed to get a message to someone in Canada who could help. Canon Jack Turner was well known and respected on Baffin Island. David had come to the right place.

Horrified at the news, Mr Cormack gave instructions to his colleague to send an emergency cable telegram with the message that Canon Jack Turner had been accidentally shot in the head and that he required urgent medical assistance by air.

The distressing broadcast made its way along the deformed telegraph wires that connected the frozen north to civilisation in the south. It was received by a radio operator in the Department of Health and Welfare in Ottawa. The message was also sent to inform Jack's clergy colleagues based in Toronto. More prayer to his Heavenly Father was needed for Jack, his wife and his two young daughters at this testing time.

The night drew on. It wasn't long before Jack's desperate situation was known throughout Canada, thanks to the radio communications of the Canadian Broadcasting Corporation.

Farmers had finished their work for the day on the vast prairies of the Canadian countryside and were sitting down to their evening meals. Staff and patients in the hospitals strewn across the land kept an ear to the daily news broadcasts that made them feel connected with the outside world. Older people in care homes also enjoyed the fruits of broadcasting as a real blessing in their lives. Radio connected people everywhere.

The news announcer brought the Turners' misfortune to the ears of the Canadian people. By God's grace, the urgent message appealing for help had made its way to the headquarters of the Royal Canadian Air Force and the Canadian Army. They would send a joint team to attempt the extremely dangerous rescue of an unknown missionary called Canon John Turner. He had been accidentally shot in the head and the bullet was stuck in his brain. Canon Turner wasn't dead, but he would die soon if he didn't receive vital medical assistance.

The missionary's house was deep in the Arctic circle. It was so remote, there were no maps for the heroic soldiers to follow. Jack's home was very far from civilised society, with all its hospitals and highly trained medical people. So, his only earthly hope rested in the intrepidness of the rescue team.

The dangerous mission was given a name. It was to be called 'Operation Canon', and it was to be put into action straight away.

Fun and Adventure

'Let's put a tent up in the back garden,' said Jack, as he stared out of his bedroom window at the gently falling rain.

'How can we put a tent up in the garden?' asked his older brother Arthur, lounging on the bed. 'We don't have a tent.'

'We'll just have to make one, won't we?' Jack replied. He turned swiftly and headed for the door. Swinging it open, he called to his mother in the kitchen downstairs.

'Mum!' he yelled.

'Yes darling?' came the sweet reply from his mother's lips.

'Can me and Arthur put a tent up in the back garden?' hollered Jack.

'Why don't you come downstairs and talk to me instead of shouting?' Ellen replied.

Jack turned his head and smiled at Arthur. He nodded in the direction of the kitchen below. Arthur jumped up from the bed and took off after his brother who had already darted down the stairs like a whippet.

'Sounds like there are elephants in the house,' mumbled Edward from the sitting room. He was the eldest boy, known by his family and friends as Ted.

Ellen was busy making sandwiches for lunch, as the two younger lads rushed in. Ellen stopped what she was doing and looked at Jack.

'Now, what was it you wanted Jack?' she asked.

'I was just wondering if we could put a tent up in the back garden, Mum?'

'That sounds like fun. But have you looked out the window? It's still raining,' said Mum, 'and we don't own a tent. That's a bit of a problem.'

'Well, I thought we could borrow your clotheshorse … and a couple of bed sheets, if that would be okay' said Jack rather sheepishly.

'And a drop of rain won't hurt us, Mum,' added Arthur.

'The lads could do with a wash!' said Ted wryly to his mother.

Mum smiled. 'I don't want either of you using my good bed sheets,' she said. 'There are some old pieces of lino[1] under the stairs you can use.'

After lunch, Ellen opened the small cupboard door under the stairs and reached in to grab hold of the lino for the tent. The boys helped her pull it out and piled

---

1. Lino is short for linoleum which is a hard, smooth, washable floor covering.

it by the back door in the yard. She noticed some old mats in there, so they were used as well.

Usually the clotheshorse was folded and perched upright behind the kitchen door. Jack found it and dragged it to the yard. The rain had stopped for now so there was no time to waste. Ted helped the two younger lads set about their task of building a camp for the night. They hadn't asked Mum if they could stay out in it all night, but they were confident she would let them.

'No, not tonight,' said Mum.

'Och Mum,' groaned Jack. 'Pleeease?'

'No, Jack, not tonight. Don't ask me anymore.'

The Turner boys were deflated, but not defeated. They would try again tomorrow and the day after that, and the day after that. Mum would give in sooner or later. She loved her boys and wanted them to be happy. Without a doubt, camping in the back garden overnight would make them very happy!

As it happens, the youngsters were right. Their determination and gritty persistence wore down their sweet mother's desire to have her sons sleep comfortably in their own beds. The makeshift tent provided the cover and comfort that they needed. When the weather was fine, the boys camped out in the garden overnight.

'It would be better to have a real canvas tent,' Jack thought. He had seen one in the town, but it was too expensive. Jack needed his brothers to help chip in for it, and they were happy to help once he told them what they were saving up for.

The boys sang in the church choir and always got a few pennies for it. That was put towards the tent fund. Sometimes they had to run some errands for Mum or do some jobs around the house for her. Mum was a generous soul and she always gave them a penny or two for their help. That money also went into the tent fund.

It wasn't very long before the lads had saved up enough money to buy the small canvas tent they so dearly wanted. It was much more comfortable than the old makeshift one they had put up in the garden. It kept the rain out too!

So, Mum got her clotheshorse back when the Turner boys pitched their new acquisition at the bottom of the garden. In fact, during the long summer months, when school children were off on holiday, the young explorers kipped many a night under the moon and stars that shone down on the quiet street in Felixstowe where they lived.

Mum didn't mind so much giving permission for Ted, Arthur and Jack to sleep overnight in their new waterproof shelter during the summertime. She had peace of mind, knowing where the boys were and what they were up to, during those summer nights in the garden. They were good lads and Ellen was devoted to her family.

However, all children can be mischievous at times and the Turner trio were no different. Jack had a disarming smile that got him out of a lot of trouble. Ellen couldn't be cross with her youngest son for too long when he grinned at her. This proved very useful to Jack.

Jack wasn't very serious about God or church at this stage in his young life, but he went to Sunday School and Bible class with his brothers because it pleased their mother.

'Look what I've got,' Jack whispered to Arthur as he pulled his hand out of his trouser pocket. It was a brass metal tack that was used for pinning pictures to the over-used cork boards scattered around the walls of the church hall. Jack found it on the floor as he was walking into the Sunday School class.

'Are you gonna hand it in to the teacher?' asked Arthur.

'Nah,' came the reply.

Jack beamed playfully. 'Do you dare me to put it on the teacher's seat when he gets up?'

'Aye, I dare you,' smirked the prankster's brother.

Jack waited patiently for the opportune moment. It came just shortly before the class was due to end. His teacher rose from his seat to have a brief word with a colleague who was sitting at a table in the far corner of the hall.

Jack moved swiftly and silently. The trap was set, and the victim was unaware. As soon as the teacher sat back down on his chair, he felt the searing pain of a metal pin pierce the upper back part of his right thigh. Oh, the pain! Oh, the laughter from the class! That was even better than his last prank of a pool of water on the seat.

Mrs Turner was deeply distressed to hear of her son's poor behaviour in Sunday School. She would rebuke him firmly, but Jack always took her scolding with a disarming smile. It dispelled her anger every time. How could she be cross at such a beautiful boy?

Ellen did not find it easy raising three energetic young men on her own. Her husband, Thomas, had died just four months before Jack was born in 1905. Ted was only five years old and Arthur was only three when it had happened. The Turners had had to move from London to Felixstowe and had taken up residence at the home of Ellen's parents.

The house was small and could only further accommodate Mrs Turner and the two youngest boys. Ted had to stay with nearby relatives. It was awful being torn apart like that, but at least they could see Ted every day. When the boys' grandmother died in 1912, the Turners moved into another home large enough to bring the family together under one roof. Ted, Arthur and Jack became inseparable.

Their playground was the beautiful countryside of the east Suffolk coast that surrounded the River Deben. The river twisted this way and that through the land for miles and miles.

The marshlands around the river provided the perfect hunting ground for young explorers. Often the Turner boys whittled bows and arrows from the reeds of the marshes and, with a friend from next door, stalked whatever wildlife they could find.

Their expeditions to hunt their game would go on for a very long time through the smelly and difficult landscape of swamps and dykes[2] to hunt their game. There were many different species of birds that gathered and nested around the River Deben throughout the year. Birds would be their prey, as you certainly never found bears roaming about the marshes.

'Just imagine what it would be like, hunting a bear!' thought Jack, as the four huntsmen crouched low in the reeds, bows and arrows at the ready. They had caught sight of a heron perched on rock at the side of the river, about one hundred feet away from them. It was a large beautiful bird with long legs and neck, and a long bill. The bird seemed to know that the boys were near, because as they peeped over the top of the reeds, it flapped its wings and rose quickly into the air. In a moment, it was gone, much to the annoyance of the hunters.

As they watched their prey soar into the air, they realised that the thrill of the hunt had made them quite hungry. It was time to trek home. A few miles lay between them and the meal that would welcome them on their return. Jack was wet, and his feet were cold. The others told him to keep moving and he would soon feel warm. So, they made for home as fast as they could manage. Eventually four tired and dirty boys arrived back in Felixstowe.

---

2. Stone walls.

Jack had no idea that later in life, he would be hunting birds and bears to survive the icy wilds of the Polar North. His time exploring the marshes of the River Deben was great training for his future service of the Lord.

A Change of Direction

It was during his days at the secondary school in Ipswich that Jack made up his mind about his future career. He wanted to be a chemist. A surprise, considering his love for exploration, hunting and the great outdoors, not to mention his school sporting achievements of captaining the school cricket and football teams. Nevertheless, Jack's ambition was not for any of these things. He worked hard at school and when he left in the autumn of 1921, he began to follow his dream and train as a chemist in Ipswich.

It wasn't all work though. Jack liked to dance. He would often go to dances to meet people and listen to the latest music. His warm, sociable personality meant that he had plenty of friends, some of whom invited Jack to be the drummer in their local band. He had friends, he had music. All Jack needed now was to indulge in the latest fashion in society, which was to smoke. Over time he became accustomed to the habit and his preference was to smoke a pipe, much to his mother's dismay.

'Dancing. Band music. Smoking. What next?' Jack's mother would think to herself. She prayed constantly for her boys, and Jack's wayward behaviour made her all the more anxious for his wellbeing.

Prayer was important to Mrs Turner and so was the work of the local Anglican church in Felixstowe, to which she was deeply attached. Ellen brought her boys to church every week. The young Turner men got involved in different ways, but they weren't that interested in taking God or the Bible at all seriously. Imagine their astonishment when the Lord sent them a church minister who did!

A new vicar was appointed to the parish in Felixstowe, which included the church of St. Andrew, in 1925. The Rev H.B. Greene loved the Lord with all his heart, mind, strength and soul. He loved the Bible too. He devoted his life to the Lord and to the care of God's people.

As a minister, Rev Greene was especially interested in the young people of his new parish church. His longing was that they might come to know Jesus Christ as Saviour and Lord in their lives. In an attempt to get to know the younger folks, he invited them each Sunday evening to his home after the church service. Jack wasn't much interested in going to these meetings. He was nineteen when Rev Greene arrived in Felixstowe, and he was a young man in full control of his life. Jack had his own plans. He would work in Ipswich as a chemist. He would make a good living and buy a house for himself. Maybe he would get married and have children. Time would tell.

Arthur and Jack would keep going to church, even though neither of them cared very much for Rev Greene's evangelical preaching. It seemed to them that Rev Greene took God and his Word much too seriously. One Sunday morning an announcement was made in the morning gathering at Felixstowe parish church, which confirmed this view.

The church was to have a Mission! This was an opportunity for Christian people to invite their friends and neighbours to hear someone tell them all about the love of God. It would be a time for men, women and children to decide who is king of their lives. Would they say sorry for their sins and follow Christ as King?

Mr Reginald Naish[1] was invited to come and tell the people of Felixstowe about Jesus. He would explain to the congregation what the Bible taught about the return of Jesus Christ to earth. Mr Naish was very glad to receive the invitation from Rev Greene. So, in December 1925 many people gathered in the church hall of St Andrew's to listen to him.

Jack wasn't interested in Jesus' return and he certainly had no plans to go to any of the meetings to hear the guest preacher. However, one night he

---

1. Reginald Naish was an experienced minister of the gospel and Christian author. He was known as a humble man who devoted himself to prayer and the Word of God, the Bible.

was passing the church hall in the rain. He heard loud singing coming from the meeting. So, he decided to duck in through the door and sat in an empty chair at the back of the room.

Jack noticed how intently everyone listened to what Mr Naish was saying. He couldn't help noticing the joy on the face of the speaker. It was very clear that this man loved the Lord Jesus and he wanted everyone else there to love Jesus too. 'And one day, when we do not expect it, the Lord Jesus Christ will come back again, and take all those who love him to be with him for ever in heaven. Will you be one of them? Are you ready to meet Jesus? Are you ready for his return?'

Jack realised that he wasn't ready to meet the Lord Jesus. He didn't know him in the same way that Mr Naish or Rev Greene did. In fact, Jack didn't know Jesus at all. Imagine going to church all his life, and not realising that it was all about Jesus!

When the meeting was over, Jack caught the attention of two other friends from church. They seemed to be interested in what they heard about Jesus Christ that evening, in the same way that Jack was.

'Do either of you know where Mr Naish is staying?' asked Jack.

'He's staying with Mr Smith,' came the reply.

'At White Lodge?' Jack retorted. 'I need to speak more with him. You two coming with me?

The lads looked at each other, then nodded affirmingly at Jack.

It was getting very late in the evening, but the three men were determined to understand more of this wonderful message from Mr Naish.

Although tired from the evening's activities, Mr Naish received his visitors very warmly. With the Bible open, Reginald began to speak with them of their need for forgiveness. He told them that on the cross, the Lord Jesus was earning forgiveness for all those people to whom he would give it as a gift.

'Jesus' blood was shed on the cross for the forgiveness of your sins. Did you know that?' he asked the young men. Their silence allowed for Naish to say more.

'Jesus said that he didn't come to us to be served, but to serve and to give his life as a ransom for many. Gentlemen, the fact that God did not spare his only Son but offered him up freely so that we could be forgiven shows the importance of forgiveness in the mind of God,' said Mr Naish.

He continued. 'Why would God have let his only Son die on the cross, if being a good person was enough to get you into heaven? If ever the idea that being decent was not good enough, lads, it is clearly shown in the death of the Lord Jesus Christ on the cross.'

'Do you know that Christ Jesus died for you? When Jesus died on the cross, he took the punishment that your sins deserve. Do you know that he is coming back again to take his people to be where he is for ever?'

As young men, Jack and Arthur didn't like sermons very much in church. They seemed to go on and on, which made them feel very bored. Jack assumed that he would be told to be good and he wasn't much interested in that. He liked fun and adventure. But that night in the sitting room of White Lodge with Mr Naish, he began to remember that Rev Greene had said similar things to the congregation since his arrival in Felixstowe.

'Jesus Christ died on the cross for me. But why?' thought Jack. No matter how hard he tried, Jack couldn't think of a good enough reason that Christ should go to a cruel cross and die in his place and for his sins. That evening for the first time in his life, Jack understood that Christianity is all about Jesus and being forgiven by Jesus.

He was not alone, for the two men who went with him to speak with Mr Naish that night, understood it too. Just as the clocks in the town were striking the hour of midnight, the three young men knelt in the sitting room of White Lodge and committed their lives to Jesus Christ.

From that wet December night in 1925, five days before Christmas, Jack's life was never to be the same again. He knew a deep and satisfying joy in his heart that he had not known before. Jack was now determined to live his life fully for Christ. But before they left the warmth of White Lodge, Mr Naish opened the Bible at 2 Corinthians 5:17 – 'Therefore, if anyone is in Christ, he is a new creation. The old has passed away; behold the new has come!'

Jack was a new creature with only one goal in life – to bring glory to God and to serve the Lord with every ounce of energy and strength he could gather. From that moment on, Jack would follow the Lord Jesus until the day he died.

Preparation for Service

Jack had a spring in his step. His love for the Lord Jesus grew day by day as he gave himself to studying the Bible and to prayer. Jesus promises to be with his people until the end of time and Jack knew deep in his heart that he would never be alone. It was such a wonderful feeling to know that he was a new man – he was a forgiven man. Jack thanked Jesus every day for his grace to him. Jack knew that he didn't deserve it, but that is the nature of God's grace – mercy, forgiveness and love to those who don't deserve it, but who turn to Christ in repentance and faith.

Going to church took on a new meaning. Jack was no longer bored listening to sermons. He had struggled with that in the past. He used to play counting games. Sometimes he would count the number of people in each pew and then try to work out how many people were in church that morning. It was always a bit more difficult to do this if his mother sat further up the church, because when Jack would crane his neck round to count those behind him, the minister would know that he wasn't listening! So, one of those occasions when he was closer to the front, he would play a different counting game called 'how many organ pipes are there?'.

Now that Jack knew he belonged to Christ, he truly wanted to hear the sermon. He wanted to learn how he could grow in his knowledge and love of God. He wanted to hear how he could best love the Lord and his people. He longed to understand his place in God's church as a servant of Christ. Jack's desire to serve the Lord was given a clear direction when Rev Greene invited his former colleague from Liverpool, Rev Daniel Bartlett, to come to church and speak to the congregation about serving Jesus around the world.

In 1922, Rev Bartlett became the General Secretary of a new mission organisation called the Bible Churchmen's Missionary Society (BCMS). It is known as Crosslinks today. Its motto was a verse from the last book of the Bible: 'for the Word of God and for the testimony of Jesus Christ' (Revelation 1:9). This verse described the clear purpose of the newly formed BCMS. The Bible would be central to its ministry, and proclaiming 'Christ crucified' would be its chief aim.

When the invitation arrived in the BCMS office in London from Rev Greene, it was received with great delight and responded to immediately. Rev Bartlett loved to visit churches. He travelled all over the country to tell people the good news of Jesus Christ and he would challenge people to consider serving the Lord

overseas as missionaries with the BCMS. Little did Jack
know that the day of Rev Bartlett's visit, 26th March
1926, would change his life for ever.

'The command to take the gospel of Jesus Christ
to every nation is still urgent,' said Rev Bartlett to the
gathered multitude. 'The need to proclaim the one
unchanging gospel of Christ in a way that connects with
people of different cultures and backgrounds and ages
is a constant challenge to Christ's church. But how will
they hear of the Saviour's love, if no one will bring the
gospel message to them? My friends, the apostle Paul
says in Romans chapter 10 verses 13-15: "'For everyone
who calls on the name of the Lord will be saved." How
then will they call on him in whom they have not
believed? And how are they to believe in him of whom
they have never heard? And how are they to hear without
someone preaching? And how are they to preach unless
they are sent? As it is written, "How beautiful are the
feet of those who preach the good news!"'

As I look out at this congregation here present,
is there anyone here with beautiful feet? Is there
anyone who will take up the challenge of the gospel
and join with the BCMS in the urgent and necessary
proclamation of salvation to the ends of the earth
through repentance and faith in Jesus Christ our Lord?'

Jack's heart was pounding in his chest. He slowly
turned to look at Arthur sitting beside him on his
right. As their gaze met, immediately they knew what
each other was thinking. Arthur also loved Jesus and it

seemed that now was time for the Turner brothers to take this whole Christian thing more seriously. There were others in the crowd that day who would, like the Turner boys, step forward in complete and glad surrender of their lives for full time Christian service overseas with BCMS.

It was usual for anyone thinking of serving the Lord overseas to be interviewed for their suitability to the momentous charge of being a missionary with the BCMS. Arthur and Jack made the journey to London to fulfil the application requirements of the Society. Having been found suitable, on 6th April 1926, Arthur was offered a place at the college, and Jack got his offer the following day. They would start training in the autumn that year.

The Bible Churchmen's Missionary and Theological College was based in Bristol, a city in south west England. Arthur and Jack started their training in October 1926 with fear, nervousness, and a little bit of excitement thrown in. However, Jack was setting himself a tremendous task. When he left school, he wanted to study chemistry. He had started training for that career in Ipswich. Jack loved it and he really wanted to be a qualified chemist. He also really wanted to serve God in a foreign land. He was determined to do both. He thought that being a fully qualified chemist would be a great help to him in his role as a missionary. Jack decided that while he was at the BCMS college, he would also attend chemistry lectures in another college nearby. He had to work very hard indeed but in the end it was worth it. Not only did Jack manage to qualify as a chemist, he also graduated from the BCMS college and was ready for his ordination as a minister in the Church of England.

When Jack arrived at the college in 1926, neither he nor his brother Arthur knew where in the world they would serve the Lord, until a visitor came from Canada. He was Bishop Stringer of Yukon, a small region in western Canada. He was at the college in Bristol to tell the students and staff about the wonderful people of the Arctic who needed to hear the gospel of Jesus Christ. They were known as the Inuit. The permanent darkness of the Arctic winter, the icy rugged wilds of the land and temperatures dropping as low as minus 60 degrees Celsius during severe blizzards, would challenge any ardent outdoor adventurer. Scattered up and down the Arctic coastline were small populations of Inuit people, living in ignorance of Jesus Christ. Missionaries would experience isolation from the world, as a ship from England would call just once a year to the area. The only way of getting around at speed was by dog sledge. And missionaries had to be hunters like the rest of the Arctic population. Could they eat raw meat? Well, not to worry, they would learn how. And they'd need to learn how to handle a rifle because polar bears were not soft and cuddly. One swipe of their claws could kill. Oh yes, they would also need to learn the Inuktitut language to communicate with the locals.

'Any volunteers?' asked the Bishop as he looked at the bewildered faces of the young crowd before him. Not surprisingly, the room was silent.

Shortly after the Bishop's visit, Arthur and Jack made their way to the principal's office. Together they had prayed about serving the Lord in the Arctic and they now had no doubt in their minds that they would go and tell the Arctic people of the wonderful salvation that is offered by Christ to anyone who would repent and believe in him. They hoped Dr Carter, the college Principal, would receive this news positively. It was Dr Carter's responsibility to ensure that every student received the proper training for life in the mission field. He also wanted to expose his students to worldwide possibilities for Christ's service and would on occasion invite guests, such as Bishop Stringer, into the college to address the college population and enlighten them to gospel needs around the world. He was delighted to hear that the Turner brothers were offering themselves for service in the Arctic.

In a report to Rev Dr Bartlett (as he became known) at BCMS headquarters in London, Dr Carter said that Jack was 'a most simple earnest Christian with a lovable disposition, and he will be ready to work wholeheartedly with anyone and anywhere. He seems very strong and should be able to stand any sort of climate quite well.'

On the 26th June 1928, at the age of twenty-six, Arthur Turner set sail for Pangnirtung, on the southern tip of Baffin Island in the Arctic. Baffin Island is the third largest island in the world. Jack would follow his brother to the same island the following year.

Before going abroad, Jack wanted to make the most of his time left at home and there was something that he wanted to do. He knew that there was a meeting held every year in the town of Keswick, a beautiful little town surrounded by mountains and lakes in northern England. The meeting was called the Keswick Convention and thousands of Christian people from all over the world would meet in large tents to hear Bible teaching, sing hymns of praise, and make new friends. Jack wanted to go there as further preparation for the Lord's service overseas. The only problem was, Jack had no money to pay his expenses. To his mind, this was only a small problem. He grabbed two bed sheets and dipped them in paraffin wax and linseed oil. This made them waterproof. Jack would use them to make a tent. He needed food, some changes of clothes and transport. Again, this was no problem as he had a bicycle. The journey was three hundred miles or so. Jack reckoned that it would take him a few days to get to the convention. He would simply pitch his tent at the side of the road to sleep at night, and cycle as much as he could by day.

When everything was ready, Jack loaded the tent, food and clothes on to his bicycle and set off on the long journey. He slept by the roadside for two nights and on the third day he reached his destination. As he was coming into the town Jack could see tents dotted all over the green fields. There were hundreds of young people camping under canvas and he found a suitable place to pitch his shelter.

The week passed too quickly as far as Jack was concerned. He felt blessed and his heart was bursting with joy. He loved meeting new people and talking about Jesus. He loved the Bible teaching that fed his soul. He sang his heart out with the hundreds of worshippers around him at the meetings. He encouraged people to pray for him as he embarked as a servant of Christ on his Master's mission, to seek and to save the lost in the freezing conditions of the Arctic.

The morning of his return, Jack set his mind to climbing the local mountain. Skiddaw is the sixth highest peak in England and Jack wanted to reach its heights before the sun came up. He would leave once he took in the majesty and splendour of the sunrise. As the sun rose over the horizon, Jack praised God the Creator for the beauty of his world.

He descended to the field where his belongings were. He packed up his kit on to his bicycle and headed for home. It only took two days and one roadside sleepover to get back to Felixstowe.

Not long after, Jack wanted to take one last trip up the River Deben on a sailboat. He had a small posse of children with him and the weather seemed favourable. The river was teeming with birdlife as usual and the crew enjoyed the sights and sounds of their surroundings. Suddenly, a freak wind took the sail by surprise and forced the boat to turn over. All the occupants were thrown into the water. Six of them were able to swim safely to the bank of the river, but Jack and one child became entangled in the sail. Jack knew how dangerous their plight was. The sail was beginning to wrap itself around the thrashing pair of bodies; they were gasping for breath. Jack was strong and he managed to free himself from the sail. He turned his attention immediately upon his fellow sufferer. Jack heaved the sodden sail with all his might and grabbed hold of the child's flailing arms. Once completely free from the sail, they swam to the edge of the river, realising that they had escaped a tragic end.

Later, as Jack thought about that day in the boat, he felt sure that God had spared his life for the Inuit people of the Arctic to whom he would bring the gospel of Christ. It was another sign of God's blessing in his life.

Journey to the Arctic

The ship creaked and moaned as it slowly pushed its way through the icy waters of Hudson's Bay in northern Canada. Jack was lying in his bed staring at the ceiling of his cabin. He listened to every groan the boat made as it scraped up against the icebergs floating past. He didn't want to get up. It was warm in bed and his cabin was cold. In just a few hours, the boat would finally dock at Pond Inlet, a small community living on the northern shores of Baffin Island in the Arctic. This would be his home and the place where he would begin his work for the Lord in that majestic and mysterious land.

He thanked the Lord for bringing him safely there. He thanked the Lord for his companion, Harold Duncan, who would share this ministry to the Inuit. Just a couple of months previously, in the summer of July 1929, he and Harold were ordained by Bishop Farthing in a small church known as Christ Church, in Aylmer, Quebec. The service was a wonderful occasion and when it was over, the two men were guests of honour at a reception given by the Women's Auxiliary of the Mission Society of the Church of England in Canada. Those present took to their hearts the two young men who would give up a comfortable life in Britain, to travel to a tough place and endure many hardships in service of the Lord Jesus Christ. The day after the church service, they set sail for Baffin Island on the *SS Nascopie*. Jack and Harold stood on the deck, waving at the crowd who had gathered to see them safely off. Jack knew that it would be a while before they would see any of their faces again, if at all.

The ship's journey was slow as it headed north. On the way, it stopped at lonely trading stations owned by the Hudson's Bay Company. So far, they were touching land where missionaries had previously served for years. Jack and Harold liked to go ashore and meet the local population. They were heartened by the eager desire of the people to have church services. Many of the Inuit in these places had heard the gospel of Christ before and had turned to love and follow Jesus. The new missionaries were brought into a hut or tent on the shore and all who had gathered would sing praises to God and hear the Bible explained. Harold was very musical, and his accordion went with him to every meeting, much to the delight of the local congregation.

Jack was deeply encouraged that the local people welcomed them gladly. He thought that he should write home and tell his mother how things had been going so far. It was good that he loved writing, because it was usual for BCMS missionaries to keep diaries of their work and write letters to send home to England.

Jack sat at the tiny desk in his cabin. The gas lamp was perched on a narrow shelf above the desk. It gave enough light for Jack to see what he was writing. He started to tell of the weather conditions and how cold it was. Ice everywhere. Snow too. The journey was very slow going. Then he relayed the stories of the church meetings that they were able to hold, and one in particular warmed his heart: 'There were about fifty to sixty natives present,' Jack wrote, 'and the service was held in the Hudson's Bay Post Manager's House, where the natives always go for worship. They all seemed to enter into the meaning of the service and the singing was sweet. I feel a greater love for the Inuit each time I go amongst them; they are a most lovable people.'

Jack promised to write more and told his mother how much he loved and missed her, and that she should not worry, for his Heavenly Father watches over all his children.

The *SS Nascopie* pushed north until it reached the southern tip of Baffin Island and docked at a place called Lake Harbour. It was here that a Christian Inuit man boarded with his family. David Sandy was tasked to work with Jack and Harold in Pond Inlet, at least for the first year of their gospel mission. He would prove to be a very helpful man, as he taught the missionaries the ways of the local people.

The vessel steamed on to Southampton Island situated west of Lake Harbour and picked up some more passengers. One of them was a young lad called Ben. Up until recently Ben had been at school in Canada. Sadly, he had been unwell, so the school thought it best for him to return home to Southampton Island. His dad wanted Ben to continue his education and made an arrangement with Jack and Harold that Ben would go with them to the new mission house in Pond Inlet. Ben would help them get to grips with the difficult Inuit language and, in return, the men would assist Ben with his studies. It was a good arrangement.

When he had finished praying, he jumped up and quickly put on his outdoor clothes. He was going up on deck to see if land was near! Harold was already standing at the front of the ship when Jack appeared beside him. They were wearing thick coats and hats, to help keep out the Arctic cold.

'I can't believe that we are nearly there, after all these weeks at sea,' said Harold. 'The captain said that we should be at Pond Inlet by the middle of the afternoon.'

'That'll give us some time to start building the mission house,' said Jack. 'We should get a few hours of daylight today and with the help of the crew over the next couple of days, it shouldn't take too long to get the house built.'

'My hands are cold, Jack. I don't think it'll be easy to hold the tools, but I will do my best.'

'We both will,' assured Jack, patting Harold on the shoulder.

As the men stood looking out for the shoreline of Pond Inlet, they saw the long-twisted tusk of a strange looking whale poking up through the glassy surface of the water. They were told that narwhals swam in the Arctic seas, but they'd not seen one before. Such an amazing sight. In fact, throughout the *SS Nascopie's* journey north from Quebec to Baffin Island, it was usual to watch seals playing in the waters around the hull of the ship. On occasion a walrus would make an appearance for the seafarers. Jack praised God for his bountiful and wondrous creation.

By mid-afternoon, the boat dropped anchor off the shore of Pond Inlet. All the passengers and supplies bound for this destination needed to be ferried by a small motorboat to the land. It would make many trips back and forth that day. The wood for the new mission house needed to be unloaded too.

A group of local people gathered to see their missionaries arrive. Jack and Harold could hear them talking and laughing as the men, women and children of Pond Inlet waited to greet the newcomers. As the missionaries stood before the welcome party, it was easy to see that Harold was very much taller than Jack. The Inuit gave every newcomer a name, so they called Harold 'Angeneksak', meaning, 'the bigger one', due to his stature. They referred to Jack as 'Mikeneksak', which meant 'the smaller one', because the top of Jack's head only reached the bottom of Harold's nose! It is true that God's workers come in all shapes and sizes.

Once all the supplies and wood for the mission house was placed ashore, Jack and Harold immediately turned their thoughts to getting it built. The captain very graciously allowed some of his crew to help with the construction, but the *SS Nascopie* was setting sail in two days, so it was very important not to waste any time. The locals wanted to help too. Everyone worked very hard to get the foundation and frame of the house built. It took two days to erect. Then they watched the ship slowly steam out of the Inlet and into the distance. The men waved at the crew as they disappeared from view. It would be a year before they would see the boat again.

That week, snow started to fall, quietly covering the rocky ground of the Inlet like a thin white blanket. At night the temperature dropped below freezing. Winter was on the way. Jack and Harold found it difficult to handle the tools needed for the build, but they worked as hard as they could, despite the chilly conditions. The natives were a great encouragement to the Englishmen. Together they would finish building the house. It would have four rooms and a loft in total. The largest room would be used in a number of different ways – as a kitchen, as a room for the church meeting on Sundays, and also as the school room during the week for the local children to look at books or play board games like snakes and ladders, or do jigsaw puzzles.

Later Jack wrote to his mother about this experience of building the mission station with Harold: 'By the time the boat left we were well on with the work,' Jack said. 'After a week we were able to sleep in the loft until we had finished the outside work and our own rooms. This took five or six weeks. The natives received us warmly and showed us no little kindness. The people gathered around us very readily, eager to unite for worship and hear the Bible explained. We have visited their houses regularly and have always had a warm welcome.'

The BCMS mission station at Pond Inlet was completed two months after Jack and Harold's arrival. It was now time for them to give their full attention to the missionary work in the Arctic.

A Missionary's Life

There were many challenges in reaching the local people with the good news of Jesus Christ. Incredibly, Jack's parish was the size of England and France put together. That's a massive area to cover by dog sledge or on foot. To make it harder, there were only a few thousand people living within his parish. Inuit communities were small, usually made up of just a few families, scattered across the vast land. It was also common for people to live along the coastline of Baffin Island. Being close to the water made hunting for fish, seal, walrus and narwhal easier.

At home, the waters of the English Channel would keep swooshing back and forth along the beaches of southern England, even in the cold winter months. But not in the Arctic. Every year as winter approached, Baffin Bay would freeze over and this brought a strange silence to the ears of the English missionaries living at Pond Inlet. The sun would disappear towards the end of October and not be seen until the following February. The Polar Night, as it's known, would force oil lamps to be in constant use until the daylight returned.

The winter was a busy time of year for Jack. Even though the size of Jack's community at Pond Inlet was quite small, he had opportunity to meet a great many more people. They travelled to the settlement for the Hudson's Bay Company's trading post. There they could get many supplies in exchange for furs which the hunters had acquired from their trips. Some families travelled hundreds of miles by dog sledge and on foot to trade there. When they arrived, they pitched their tents, or built their snow houses, close to Jack's mission station. This was a wonderful time for Jack to preach the gospel of Christ to many natives. That was why he had come there after all.

Harold was musical and could play the accordion very well. He led the congregation in singing songs such as 'Jesus loves me this I know, for the Bible tells me so.' Jack prayed with them and opened the Word of God to them. He would speak tenderly of the Saviour's love for them, dying on the cross in their place and for their sins. If they placed their trust in Jesus, they need not fear the future, as Jesus gives not only forgiveness, he also gives eternal life with him in heaven. This message was new to the locals' ears. They feared everything! The Inuit believed that everything had a spirit – the sun and moon, the slain animals, the killed fish, everything. Every offended spirit needed to be appeased. The people had no peace of mind. As they got older, they also feared darkness and death. But the gospel of the crucified Christ that Jack was bringing to them was good news and many hundreds of Inuit people put their trust in Jesus and were baptised.

As the work in Pond Inlet settled, Jack made long trips to other communities in his parish, leaving Harold to get on with the daily work at the mission house. Jack spent a lot of time travelling, and he was normally accompanied by a local experienced travelling guide. The usual way to travel was by sledge pulled by a large team of fifteen or sixteen husky dogs. It was slow going and very hard work at times, especially if the ice on the ground wasn't good for sledging on. One time he wrote in his diary a description of travelling by sledge between camps.

"Soon after midday we came into very rough ice which meant plenty of warm work. We wanted to reach another snow house (igloo), so we pushed on. 'Pushed' is hardly descriptive enough; 'struggled,' 'stumbled', 'pulled', and 'sweated' are only some of the words needed to describe travelling in the dark, through rough ice and deep snow."

On long journeys, Jack needed to rest his animals and make a snow house to sleep in. When that happened, the first thing he did was unload the sledge and feed the dogs. He always travelled with food on the sledge. He would loosen the beasts from their harnesses and feed them with the frozen carcass of the seal that he had packed for the trip. When their bellies were full, the animals contented themselves to sleep in the snow, their dense fur coats protecting them from the cold. This allowed Jack the peace he needed to build his shelter for the night.

Jack would find suitably well packed snow and use his wide snow knife to cut blocks for the igloo. Soon the circular dome of the igloo would rise from the surrounding snowy flat surface. Its roof looked a little bit like a mushroom that Jack had often seen growing at the bottom of his garden in Felixstowe. If possible, Jack tried to cut each snowy block three feet long, two feet wide and four inches thick. Sometimes he had to vary the size of his blocks, especially if the condition of the snow wasn't all that good. When the house was up, Jack would pack the gaps between the blocks with snow. This snow would freeze and make the house mostly wind proof.

Crawling inside on his hands and knees, Jack would spread whatever furs he had brought with him on the floor of the igloo. This provided him with some protection from the cold surface. The light from his blubber lamp could be seen through the edges of the snow blocks of his temporary home. He would also get a bit of heat from this. It wouldn't take long for the atmosphere to warm up and for Jack to get the much-needed rest in preparation for the travelling adventures of the next day.

Time and again Jack made this temporary dwelling on his journeys from camp to camp. He became very good at building snow houses, even for an Englishman!

While Jack was away, Harold Duncan continued the task of visiting the locals and visitors, to speak with them about Jesus Christ. Each evening he would leave the warmth of the mission house stove and brave the icy wilds of the night. Visits were usually made in the evenings because the men were out hunting during the day. As soon as the boys are old enough, they go hunting with their fathers too. They learn how to build snow houses and shacks for shelter. They learn how to train and drive the dogs with the sledges. So the missionaries made their visits in the evenings, as it was important to meet the whole family.

On arriving at a snow house, Harold would crawl through the low tunnelled entrance into the circular and domed chamber. It wasn't easy for Harold being so tall, but he managed it nonetheless. The family would sit cross-legged, making room for Harold to sit. As there was no ventilation in the igloo, he found the atmosphere hot and rank. He wasn't used to seeing and smelling raw seal blubber lying about the room. He could never work out if it was remnants of dinner, or preparation for the next day's meal. Not the sort of thing he was used to back in England. But he reminded himself that he was a missionary compelled by the love of Christ. He quickly forgot about his surroundings as he spent a joyous evening in the company of kind and hospitable people.

Some portions of the Bible had been translated into the local Inuktitut language many years before by a missionary called Dr Edmond Peck. Harold would pull some of these books out of his pockets and together read the Bible and sing songs of praise to God, as outside the meeting, the biting wind whistled its way through the wintry wonderland.

The missionaries wanted the Inuit to be able to read the Bible for themselves in their local language. An invitation was given to anyone in Pond Inlet to come to the mission station in the evenings and there they would be taught to read and write. They would hear Bible stories and commit passages to memory. The Inuit were very good at remembering stories and found it easy to learn chapters and even some books of the Bible.

It wasn't easy for Jack to learn Inuktitut. His old BCMS College Principal said that he was 'a hard and most conscientious worker and a real plodder ... a most simple earnest Christian with a lovable disposition.' It's okay being a plodder, especially if you're a hard-working conscientious type! Jack had plodded to train to be a scientist, he had worked hard to finish training at the BCMS College, but he wasn't a natural linguist. Let's not forget that Inuktitut was renowned for being a difficult language to master, even more so than Russian or Swedish or Greek! Nonetheless, during the cold days, while the men went out to hunt, Jack threw himself into studying the Arctic tongue for hours each day. He found Ben an incalculable help with learning to speak and write Inuktitut. Jack was determined to do it so fluently that he could preach the gospel of Christ in Inuktitut. Eventually he wanted to translate parts of the Bible into Inuktitut – those parts that Dr Peck had not managed to get around to.

Jack thought it was a strange looking language. The written language was invented by a Canadian Methodist minister called John Evans, back in 1840. On paper, it looked like triangles and circles, squiggles and letters, but when they were put together, they formed words. Jack just had to learn what each meant. He would do what he did best; work hard and plod on. With God's help Jack knew that he would get there in the end.

One Christmas Jack invited some young people into his home for some food and fun. He handed out blank pieces of paper and announced that they would have a Scripture competition. He was keen to know just how much of the Bible they had actually learnt during his time with them. Jack called out a verse of the Bible and they had to write down which book of the Bible it came from, which chapter it was from, and even the verse number. He read out thirty-two verses and the winner got eighteen right! Very impressive, thought Jack. I'll keep my eye on that one. He could be a church leader one day!

Jack did encounter some difficulties translating passages of the Bible into Inuktitut. The landscape of the Polar North is quite barren. There are no trees or cornfields. There are some animals that are not found wandering around the vast open plains of the Arctic, such as sheep or oxen. There were no local words for these, so it was hard to help people understand those stories in the Bible that speak of such things, like the parable of the Wheat and the Tares, or Jesus speaking of himself as the Good Shepherd. Thankfully, Jack had some Bible pictures in his study, which made an appearance when the time was needed.

During his ministry in the Arctic, Rev Turner translated a number of Old Testament books for publication. He revised the New Testament that Dr Peck had translated into Inuktitut many years before. He had a lot of Scriptural chorus songs transformed into the local language. And, as an Anglican minister, he had almost completed a translation of the Book of Common Prayer too. Indeed, Jack was a hard and most conscientious worker and a real plodder. Nothing wrong with that.

On the Trail

As the winds picked up speed and force, Jack and his guide scrummaged forward like rugby players, claiming every inch a victory. 'One step closer to bringing the gospel of Jesus to a lost soul,' Jack thought to himself. He had stepped off his sledge to make it easier for his hungry dogs to pull the heavy load. They were weak with hunger. The food supply had run out and Jack needed to hunt for more. A meal was hard to find in the blizzard at Pangnirtung Fiord. He prayed earnestly that the Lord would grant him, his native companion and their animals the strength to make it to the next camp.

'It's time to stop,' he shouted to his guide. The words were carried away by the ferocious wind. Holding on to the reins of the sledge, Jack ran to his companion and touched his shoulder.

'Let's make camp here,' he shouted, pointing to the ground. Jack's sledge had broken on the journey through rough ice. He would mend it and build a snow house. It's very hard building anything in strong winds, but his native friend was a good help. He cut the snow blocks as Jack built the house. It was warm work. The house grew slowly with each block of snow, until they were able to crawl inside for shelter from the stinging wind. Jack encouraged himself by remembering the Bible verse that he had read that morning – Proverbs 3:24. 'If you lie down, you will not be afraid; when you lie down, your sleep will be sweet.'

As the night went on, the walls of the igloo took a severe battering from the gale outside. They knew it wouldn't be long before the snow blocks would be worn through by the wind. By morning, the house that Jack built was half full of snow. It didn't manage to keep the cold out, so the two men began the day in great discomfort. After breakfast, it was time to press on.

They were travelling to small communities near Pangnirtung. Jack had been asked to cover his brother Arthur's mission station there, during Arthur's furlough back in England. Harold Duncan was in Pond Inlet, holding the fort for Jack. It was usual for Jack to travel as far as he could to bring the gospel of Jesus Christ to as many people in the Arctic as he could. The weather and poor travelling conditions would not deter him from this mission. He was compelled by the love of Christ to keep looking for people who did not know the good news of the love of Christ and share the gospel of grace with them.

The biting winds and snowy blizzards made travelling tough going. As the men pushed on, it was clear to them that they would have to leave one sledge and most of their load on the trail.

'Which one is better?' asked Jack. 'I've repaired mine a few times. Perhaps yours?'

His companion nodded in agreement. They set to work harnessing all the dogs together into one team. They packed only the essentials onto the guide's sledge and abandoned the rest.

'This should make things easier,' Jack said.

Good progress was made with the lighter sledge and bigger dog team. But the dogs were skinny and not as strong as they had been when they set out on their journey back in Pangnirtung just over a week before.

One morning the weather abated and made travel easier but, by the afternoon, things became dire. The snow was thick and deep on the frozen bay. Travelling over frozen water was safer as you avoided hitting any rocks concealed by the snow. Jack discovered that the weight of the snow pushed the salty water up through the seal holes. These holes were created by the seals so that they could come up for air when swimming in the frozen ocean. As Jack's sledge passed slowly through the snow, the salt water below stuck to the sledge runners, making travel very laborious, if not impossible, for the men and their dogs. They reached a little island and decided to stop and set up camp.

'My feet are soaking,' said Jack. 'My sealskin boots didn't keep the water out. If I stand still to make the igloo, they will freeze, and I will be in trouble. I don't want frostbite.'

'I'll make the snow-house,' his companion said. 'You keep walking about to stop your feet from freezing. Make sure you stomp your feet.'

Jack stamped up and down while the igloo was being built. He needed to keep the blood circulating in his feet. It's a bad sign if they become numb. Once the house was ready, Jack crawled inside and took off his boots. It wasn't long before light from their blubber lamps filled the dome of the igloo. Jack looked carefully at his toes. He counted ten, so that was a good sign! They looked okay to him. There was still some distance to go before the next village, and he needed all his toes. He praised God quietly for keeping him from frostbite.

After eating, he slid into his sleeping bag and snuggled down for some well-earned rest. He began to warm up a bit more and soon he was asleep. The dogs were outside the igloo, lying in the snow, their thick fur coats providing the protection they needed from the nippy winds.

The next morning, Jack and his guide pushed on through the fresh snow. The winds had dropped a bit, so they were able to make a good distance during the days to follow. Although the dogs were tired, skinny and in desperate need of food, they pulled the sledge as best they could. The men kept on the lookout and hunted when the opportunity arose. Some excursions were more successful than others.

Eventually they arrived at a small village where they were warmly greeted by the families who lived there. The Inuit people are very generous and gladly share whatever they have to ease the discomfort of weary travellers. The men and their dogs were fed and watered when they arrived that first evening there. The following day, Jack sent his companion off with some of the local men on a hunting trip. While they were away, Jack took every opportunity he could to preach and teach the gospel of Christ to every Inuit person who was willing to hear. He wanted every man, woman, boy and girl to hear of the Saviour's love for them and to sing God's praises. By now he was getting familiar with the local language and as the people gathered, he began to teach them one of his favourite Christian songs: 'Jesus loves me, this I know'. Such a simple song, Jack thought, but filled with truth about Jesus.

Jack sang the first line and the congregation repeated it. Then the second line, and the third. It wasn't long before they were singing joyfully together:

Jesup nagligingmanga	Jesus loves me, this I know,
Iilaa qaujimavunga	For the Bible tells me so;
Suli uqaujjaugama	Little ones to him belong,
Godipuqausinginni	They are weak, but he is strong.
Iilaa Jesusip	Yes, Jesus loves me,
Nagligivaanga	Yes, Jesus loves me,
Uvanga iilaa	Yes, Jesus loves me,
Nagligillaaqpaanga	The Bible tells me so.

Jesup nagligiplunga	Jesus loves me, he who died
Tuqqutigilauqpaanga	Heaven's gate to open wide;
Piijarumagamigit	He will wash away my sin,
Ajunrnikka tamaita	Let his little child come in.
Iilaa Jesusip	Yes, Jesus loves me,
Nagligivaanga	Yes, Jesus loves me,
Uvanga iilaa	Yes, Jesus loves me,
Nagligillaaqpaanga	The Bible tells me so.
Taamnalu suungugami	Gentle Jesus, with me stay
Kamaginiaqpaanga	Close beside me all the way;
Uivirijauguma	When at last I come to die
Qiksalirumaluunnit	Take me home with you on high.
Iilaa Jesusip	Yes, Jesus loves me,
Nagligivaanga	Yes, Jesus loves me,
Uvanga iilaa	Yes, Jesus loves me,
Nagligillaaqpaanga	The Bible tells me so.

Jack smiled warmly as the people sang the song. When he spoke of the Saviour's love for them, they listened carefully to every word. Over the few days that Jack was with them teaching the Bible, many of the people put their trust in the Lord. Jack's heart was greatly gladdened by their desire to follow Jesus. After all, that was why he and his brother Arthur came to their land as missionaries.

A man and woman approached Jack during his first day in their camp. There was sadness in their eyes. They wanted Jack to follow them to their home. There was someone that they wanted him to meet.

The three of them made their way through the snow until they stopped at a small wooden shelter, close to where the people had gathered for the service. As the man pushed the door open, light shone into the darkened room. Jack could see a small sealskin bed on the floor, with a young boy lying on it. He was very sick. On the wall opposite the bed was a little window. It was opened so that the lad could hear what was going on outside.

The missionary knelt by his bed. He could see that the boy was skinny and coughing badly. There were beads of sweat on his brow. Jack had seen this sickness before. It was tuberculosis, a terrible infection of the lungs. If it wasn't treated early, the disease would cause death. Jack looked into the boy's eyes. He could see that the sickness had taken hold of him. There was little Jack could do to help the boy's physical recovery.

He prayed with all his might, that the Word of God, which the boy could hear through the little open window, would heal his soul. 'O Lord grant that it may,' Jack thought.

The following day, Jack left the camp. He never found out what had happened to the boy.

Returning Home

At the mission house in Pond Inlet, Jack was getting ready to return home to England. 'The *SS Nascopie* will be here tomorrow,' Jack said, as he loaded a duffle bag with some of his treasured books.

'Have you got everything you need packed in your bags?' asked Harold, from his chair next to the stove.

'Yes, I think so,' said Jack. 'Are you going to be okay here on your own for the year?'

'I managed alright while you were looking after Arthur's place. I'll be fine. The Lord watches over his people,' said Harold.

'Amen to that!' exclaimed Jack. 'I'm really going to miss this place.'

'And we will miss you. But you'll have a wonderful opportunity to be with your mum. Pass on my sincere regards to her and to Ted.'

'Will do,' said Jack. 'Did I tell you that it was Ted who taught me to sail? He did a stint in the Royal Navy Volunteer Reserve during the Great War. When he came home, he imparted his sailing expertise to Arthur and me. Looking back, I can see how wonderfully the Lord was preparing us for life here.'

'Without a doubt,' laughed Harold.

The snow was falling quietly outside the house. Jack stared through the lounge window at the partially frozen bay. Everything was still. He could not hear any noise outside.

Inwardly Jack felt the mixed emotions of happiness and sadness. He was happy to be going back to England to see his family. It was three years since he got a hug from his mother and he couldn't wait to tell his brother Ted of his hunting trips on the bay waters of Baffin Island in a kayak. He was looking forward to telling his church family all about the people on Baffin Island. He was sad to leave his precious Inuit for the year. Jack had grown to love them very dearly. It was worth every effort he could muster, to bring them the wonderful message of Jesus. But it was time to go home for a while.

The *SS Nascopie* anchored in the bay the next morning. A small wooden motorboat departed from it. One man steered the boat carefully from the ship's side to the shoreline. Jack grabbed his bags and made his way to meet them. Some of the villagers gathered at the water's edge to bid Jack farewell. They loved him and hoped that he would hurry back to them.

Jack threw his bags into the boat. The sailor started to push the boat away from the shore with Jack's help. When they were clear, they jumped in. The sailor started up the small engine that would propel the boat back to the ship. Jack looked at the shore to see his beloved people waving goodbye. Harold towered over them, waving vigorously and shouting, 'Goodbye Jack! Keep safe and strong in the Lord!'

It took a few months to get Jack home to England, but the journey was good. Standing outside the door of his mother's home, Jack felt like he had only been away for a short while. He knocked loudly and waited. The door creaked open. Before him stood his mother Ellen.

'Hello Ma,' said Jack warmly as he grinned from ear to ear.

'Jack!' exclaimed Ellen. She moved forward and embraced her youngest son so tightly that he could hardly breathe. 'It's so good to see you, son.'

'It's good to see you too, Ma. I've missed your hugs.'

'Come on inside and I'll pop the kettle on.'

Jack followed Ellen into the kitchen and sat down at the table in the corner.

'How long are you home for?' she asked.

'Oh, about six months. I have a number of churches to visit while I am back, to let them know how the mission is going and to thank them for their support,' said Jack. 'I've a trip to Scotland planned too,' he said. 'I'll get the train up some weekend. I'll preach and speak about the Inuit in the Arctic, then I'll travel back. But don't worry, Ma, I'll have plenty of time for you.'

Ellen turned to Jack and smiled. It was wonderful to have her son back home for a little while. She was so proud of Jack, of all her boys. They were good lads.

Jack was very conscientious and determined to meet all his supporting churches back in Britain. It was important to him that they learned of the great need for missionary work among the Inuit. He wanted to stir up a desire to support and pray for the conversion of the Arctic people.

His trip to Scotland came around quickly. Jack travelled to a church in Glasgow, a city of just over a million people at the time of his visit in 1933. There was great opportunity to speak to many people about his work for the Master. He enjoyed fellowship over a hot meal back at the minister's house. Then he made his way to the train station. He bought a ticket for the journey back south.

The ticket collector was standing by the barrier to the platform. Jack reached into his pocket and pulled out a gospel tract. This little booklet explained the gospel of Jesus, and how someone can follow him. Jack handed his train ticket to the collector and then he thrust the tract into the man's outstretched hand.

'What's this?' asked the man.

'Read it,' replied Jack. 'It will explain how you can be saved from your sins by trusting in Jesus Christ.'

The man looked sternly at Jack. 'Can't you see I'm busy? I'll read it later,' he said, as he stuffed the leaflet into his jacket pocket.

The ticket collector watched the clergyman board the train, making a mental note of the carriage Jack was seated in.

Only a few moments passed when the renowned Glaswegian evangelist, James Stewart, made his way to the ticket barrier. He was the founder of the European Evangelistic Crusade. This organisation wanted to see the gospel of Jesus proclaimed all over Europe for the salvation of people who lived within its borders.

'Tickets please,' said the ticket collector. Mr Stewart held out his ticket, along with a leaflet explaining the gospel of Jesus Christ.

'What's this?!' exclaimed the ticket collector.

'Let me urge you to read this leaflet,' said James. 'You'll understand your need for Jesus Christ if you do.'

'Not another one of you religious chaps giving away leaflets?' The collector remarked.

'What do you mean?' asked James.

'Just there now, a small chap gave me one of these things,' replied the man, as he waved the leaflet in the air.

'He's on this train?'

'Aye. He boarded that carriage over there,' the collector said, pointing to the carriage directly opposite the barrier.

Mr Stewart walked to the carriage and climbed on board. Jack was the only man in the carriage at that moment, so he was easily recognisable.

'Pardon me,' said James. 'May I ask if you gave the ticket collector a gospel tract on your way through the barrier?

'Yes, that's right,' said Jack.

'May I join you? My name is James Stewart and I am an evangelist for Christ'

'Yes indeed, how wonderful!'

James Steward sat in the seat next to Jack. 'What's your name?' James asked.

Jack smiled and said, 'Turner, Jack Turner of the BCMS Arctic Mission.'

'And tell me, what does BCMS stand for?' enquired James. 'Is that a Baptist or Brethren society?'

'It stands for the Bible Churchmen's Missionary Society,' explained Jack. 'It's a Church of England mission society.'

James looked incredulously at Jack. 'You cannot be serious,' he said in a strong Glaswegian accent. 'You cannot be a member of the Church of England and distributing tracts. I have never heard of such a thing!'

Jack laughed heartily. He was very aware that the other Christian denominations looked with suspicion on the Church of England. It was recognised as a respectable institution of society, not known for its evangelistic zeal.

'My dear Mr Stewart,' Jack said, 'I can assure you that there are many keen and faithful people in the Church of England who do such things.'

'Mr Turner, in all my days as a travelling evangelist, I have seen many strange things and I have seen many wonderful things. I have witnessed the all-consuming power of God work in the lives of men and women, boys and girls. Their hearts have been set on fire by the pure Word of God proclaimed to them and they have understood their need for God's grace.'

The pitch of his voice rose higher the more he spoke.

'I have seen people in their hundreds, bow the knee to Jesus the King. I have seen scores of people weep and wail as the Holy Spirit convicted them of their sin and brought them to the foot of the cross of Christ in repentance and faith.'

'How magnificent!' Jack thought.

James continued. 'But you are asking me to believe that there are those in the Church of England who are born again of the Spirit of God, and who want to see lost souls won for Christ, and who spend many a free day giving out the gospel message to our crooked and depraved generation?'

'Mr Stewart, that is exactly what I am asking you to believe,' said Jack, 'because it is true.'

Jack was enjoying this conversation very much. It was clear to him that it would take more to convince the young evangelist, that God's faithful people could also be found in Anglican churches. The fact that Mr Stewart had never heard of members of the Church of England giving away gospel tracts didn't annoy Jack. Although Jack could see the incredulity written on the preacher's face, he thought of something that might just help poor Mr Stewart. Jack reached up for his luggage in the rack above his head and pulled his suitcase down on to his lap. He opened it carefully to reveal his clergy robes, consisting of his surplice, scarf and hood, which all ordained ministers in the Church of England wore during services.

'Are you convinced, Mr Stewart?' asked Jack.

James couldn't believe his eyes. He might have conceded the possibility of a Church of England member giving away a gospel tract. But a clergyman of the Church of England?! Impossible!

Once again Jack smiled kindly at his new friend. He looked straight into James's face. Surely Mr Stewart was convinced now, Jack thought. After all, he had the ticket collector's testimony, the young missionary beside him, the suitcase full of clerical gear. What more does he want? Convincing proof in Jack's mind, and he could see that Mr Stewart was coming round to the idea. Jack laughed as Stewart's face broke into a grin. At this point the only thing that each thought appropriate was to praise God for his love and mercy to all!

As the train sped southwards, the two young men became better acquainted. Jack told him of his beloved Inuit, scattered all over the Arctic wilderness, in desperate need of the Saviour's love. James spoke of his compassion for all the lost souls in Europe, trying to rebuild their lives after the Great War of 1914-1918. God did marvellous work through the lives and witness of these two men, who would each recall that journey from Glasgow to London with deep affection.

Over the following weeks and months, Jack continued to visit his supporting churches that were scattered around the country. Although he didn't think it, he was a good preacher and an effective ambassador for the Bible Churchmen's Missionary Society. He was dedicated and conscientious in his work for the BCMS right up until a few weeks before he was due to sail back to Baffin Island.

One morning he came down to breakfast after a sleepless night. Ellen was preparing some tea and toast as the eggs boiled in the pot on the cooker. As Jack sat at the table, a searing pain shot up from the lower right side of his stomach. He buckled over, grabbing his gut, and yelped with the pain.

Ellen turned to see her youngest son bent over and grimacing in anguish.

'Jack, what's the matter?' she nervously asked, as she rushed to him.

'I've got this terrible pain in my tummy,' he replied.

'We'd better get you to a doctor,' Ellen said.

'Right, that's okay,' said Jack. Usually Jack was dismissive of pain. He was fit, healthy and as strong as an ox. To concede to his mum's suggestion meant that it was serious, and he couldn't ignore the pain this time.

At the local hospital Jack was seen by a doctor who quickly diagnosed he had appendicitis, a painful swelling of the appendix. The appendix is a little organ found in the lower right side of the belly. It helps to keep the body's digestive system working well. It can be dangerous if it swells up, so the best course of action is to remove it. Jack underwent the operation to remove his appendix on 12th May 1934 at Ipswich General

Hospital. He was sent home a few days later, to continue his recovery under the watchful eye of Mrs Turner.

Everything seemed to be going well, until a few days into his home recovery, Jack contracted an infection in his chest called pleurisy. It would take a while to get back to fitness.

Throughout this bout of illness, Jack was very aware that he had to return to the Arctic in only a couple of weeks. If he was going to get back there, he needed to get better soon. The doctor was not keen that Jack should travel back to the wintry climate of Baffin Island. However, Jack was determined to be on the next boat and devised a cunning plan of action to see him regain his strength and stamina for the trip.

Ellen walked into the bedroom and sat at the edge of the patient's bed.

'How's my boy feeling today?' she asked.

'I'm feeling a bit better Ma,' said Jack. 'Hey Ma, do you remember the tent that we pitched in the back garden all those years ago?'

'Oh yes, I remember. You boys spent hours in that tent. Why do you ask?'

'Just wondered if you kept it?'

'It's in the shed, I think,' said Ellen.

Jack closed his eyes. It was time for another doze. He would put his plan into action soon.

The following day, Ellen went to the shops to pick up some groceries. Jack carefully got out of bed and headed slowly to the shed. The tent was wrapped up in a ball and thrown into the corner of the shed. It was easy to retrieve. Jack rummaged about and found some tent pegs too, and a hammer. He gingerly walked to the bottom of the garden and took his time to erect the tent. He planned to spend some time each day in the tent, as preparation for his return to Pond Inlet.

Ellen couldn't believe her eyes when she returned.

'Jack, what are you doing?!' she exclaimed. 'You should be in bed.'

'Now mother don't fret. I'll just spend a bit of time each day in this lovely tent. It'll help me get ready for my trip back to the Arctic.'

What could she do? He was a grown man, with no sense at all, it seemed to her!

So, every day, Jack walked slowly down the garden and lay in his tent for a while. He was getting slowly better. He was absolutely determined to get that boat back to his beloved Inuit. He missed them so much.

A knock came to the door. It was the doctor making a surprise call to check on Jack. Instead of taking the doctor to Jack's bedroom, Ellen escorted him down the garden to a rickety old tent. The doctor was puzzled, but only for a moment.

'Hello Doc!' came a chirpy voice from under the canvas.

'Rev Turner, is that you in there? Why are you not in bed?'

'I am in bed Doc. Just not in the house.'

'But, but …' stammered the doctor.

'Don't worry, I'm doing grand. It's all good prep for getting back to the Arctic.'

The doctor got on hands and knees and shuffled his way into the tent. Mrs Turner passed his bag to him when he was inside.

'Right, Jack, let's check you over,' he said. Ellen turned on her heels and headed back to the kitchen to put the kettle on for a brew. Even if the doctor didn't want one, she certainly did.

Jack's determination to get back to the mission station at Pond Inlet won over the doctor and the committee of the BCMS, who consented to his return. Jack loved being at home. It was wonderful to see his family and friends. Yet he couldn't wait to see the people of Pond Inlet again. The journey north was long and refreshing. Jack had plenty of time to rest and get strong on the SS *Nascopie*. As soon as he landed on the shore of his mission, he was fit and very well. That evening he wrote a letter home to his mother, in which he declared, 'Thank God I am once more at Pond Inlet.'

A New Mission Station

The Arctic environment had taken its toll on Harold. By the time Jack returned to Pond Inlet, it was Harold's turn to go back to England. Only he would never see Baffin Island again. In the five years of missionary service, Harold's health had weakened due to the intense conditions of the Polar North. He planned to remain in England and seek another ministry for the Lord Jesus.

Jack continued the work at Pond Inlet alone. As a Christian, he felt it was vitally important to start every day with Bible reading and prayer. It didn't matter where he was or what he was going to do that day. He used Bible reading notes called *Daily Light upon the Daily Path*. It went with him on every trip, along with his Bible and *The Book of Common Prayer*. This was the secret of his daring and confidence during his ministry. As he listened to God's Word, he found strength to face the many trials and difficulties of his missionary life with courage and joyfulness. He prayed earnestly for someone to share the work in his parish and the Lord provided.

On 3rd September 1936, the *SS Nascopie* anchored off the coast of Pond Inlet. The little motorboat from the ship transported the Rev Maurice Sidney Flint to his new home at the mission station. Jack was very pleased to see him. They shook hands vigorously on the stony shore, then Jack led his new colleague to the house.

'Welcome to the most northerly parish of the Church of England,' said Jack as he stepped in through the front door. 'The house isn't big, but it keeps the cold out. Have you brought a rifle with you?'

'Yes,' answered Maurice. 'I think it's in my trunk.'

'Good. I am sure you have been told this already. Keep it close to you when you go out. You'll need it to hunt and to protect yourself from the bears. They can kill you in a heartbeat if you get too close to them.'

Some local men had gathered to help lift Maurice's luggage from the motorboat to the house. It was always good to meet another teacher of the Bible. They placed his luggage in the main sitting room, greeted Maurice with enthusiasm and left him to get settled into his new surroundings.

'How hard is it to learn the local language?' asked Maurice.

'It's quite hard. You will need to spend a few hours each day learning it. We'll get started as soon as the *SS Nascopie* leaves here in a day or two. I will do everything I can to help. The locals will help too,' said Jack.

'I imagine that you have learned it all by now.'

'I am always a student, Maurice. But I know enough now to translate parts of the Bible into Inuktitut. I hope to translate *The Book of Common Prayer* as well. It will really help the Inuit to know the Scriptures if I can keep going with my translation work.'

'That's incredible!' exclaimed Maurice.

'Only by the grace of God can we do anything.'

'Well said,' replied Maurice.

He opened his trunk and lifted out his rifle. 'I will need a bit more practice using this,' he said.

'You'll be an expert in no time, with the rifle and the language,' reassured Jack.

Over the following months, the two men worked hard to help the Inuit learn the gospel of Jesus Christ. Anyone who passed through Pond Inlet was invited to attend the church services at the mission house. Often the men would see the house full of people, all wanting to hear of the Master's love for them. Like his former colleague and friend Harold Duncan, Jack also knew how to play the concertina. As the music bellowed from the little instrument in his hands, he would teach Christian songs to those who had gathered in the house, so that all might praise the Father in heaven.

Jack was convinced of the need to press beyond the fringe of his parish. He wanted to go further west into the Arctic regions. He aspired to build another mission station at Moffet Inlet and had prayed earnestly about it. Should God allow him the opportunity to build a new mission at Moffet Inlet, he would be able to reach the Inuit who lived on the islands and peninsulas farther west. Maurice was settled into life at Pond Inlet and he could easily carry on with the work there. As far as Jack was concerned, it was a good time to do it.

Having received permission from the BCMS back in London, Jack set off for the new venture accompanied by a local Inuit companion in the autumn of 1937. They decided to head north-west to Arctic Bay first. It gave Jack opportunity to meet many locals camped along the east shoreline of the island. Jack used every trip that he made to tell the locals the good news of Jesus Christ. Also Jack had heard that a new radio transmitter had been installed in the trading post of the Hudson's Bay Company there and he thought he could get a look at it. He liked that sort of thing. Little did Jack know that this radio would play a vital part in his rescue ten years later.

The journey to Moffet Inlet required all of the men's skills as intrepid explorers. It was a terrible journey. Everything seemed to go wrong. The weather was bleak. The landscape was dangerous. The sledges were loaded heavily with supplies and building materials such as tools, wood and nails for the new house. The dogs struggled to pull them through the snow and ice. They had only travelled three miles when the sledge of Jack's companion wore out. They transferred everything on to Jack's and carried on. The dogs found it harder to pull such a heavy load over rough and icy ground. The snowfall was relentless too. Some days they couldn't travel any more than a mile because the weather was so bad. By the time they reached Arctic Bay on 18th November 1937, the sledge was broken, the dogs were hungry, and the men were exhausted. They stayed in Arctic Bay for a week and sorted out all the things that they needed to continue on their way to Moffet Inlet. They borrowed two new sledges, loaded them up with their gear and set off on the final leg of their journey.

Jack and his companion arrived in Moffet Inlet on 3rd December 1937. The ground was covered with deep snow and it was very cold. These were not great conditions in which to build anything. However, Jack decided to put up the store first. Within a day, the two men had built the foundation and floor of the store. The temperature had dropped to minus 42 degrees Celsius and both men found it very hard to hold their tools for the job. Yet within a week, the store was almost finished. He hadn't been able to carry enough wood for the house as well, so Jack knew that he would need to make a few trips in order to complete the mission station. It took five months for Jack to finish the task. The mission house at Moffet Inlet was dedicated to the service of the Lord in the month of May 1938. Jack handed over the work at Pond Inlet to Maurice and he moved into the newly built mission at Moffet Inlet.

Jack's efforts to bring the gospel of Christ Jesus to the Inuit within his enormous parish[1] didn't escape the notice of people in high office. September 1938

---

1. Remember, the geographical size of England and France put together.

saw Jack being awarded the Coronation Medal in recognition of 'Arctic Service'. The Coronation Medal was a personal souvenir to commemorate the coronation of George VI. A limited number were made and sent throughout the countries belonging to the British Commonwealth. It was then up to local government authorities in those countries to decide who would get one and why they got it.

The following year, in 1939, Jack received the honour of being made Canon of the Cathedral of All Saints, Aklavik, situated in the North West territories of the Arctic Diocese. He had been in the Arctic ten years and accomplished a great many things. Over an area covering hundreds of miles, many Inuit confessed their faith in Jesus Christ publicly in baptism. Christians who could read were encouraged to trade something for a New Testament. Trading was the way in which the Inuit bought things. Jack's insatiable desire to help them and win others to Christ was the driving force that compelled him for months at a time to leave the comfort of the mission station and go into the darkness to face the dangers and piercing cold of those vast icy wastelands. Whether at home or on the trail, like the Lord Jesus, Jack was never too busy, tired or in too great a hurry to spend time with just one person who came for help. More often than not, these people needed to have the truth explained simply to them, over and over again, before they could take it in.

It wasn't long before it was time for this humble servant to go on furlough again back to England. Jack arrived in Liverpool on Saturday, 28th October 1939, a month after the start of the Second World War. He couldn't wait to see his mum and brother Ted. There was so much to talk about. He had been listening intently to the British news on his little radio. He was keen to know more about the reasons for war with Germany. There were so many questions, and so much to tell his family about his own work among the Inuit.

There was one thing that puzzled the Inuit about Jack – why was he not married? Every Inuit man chose a wife as soon as he was old enough to marry, but Jack remained single. The only conclusion was that outsiders were funny people! They were not aware that Jack had given it serious thought. He knew well enough how valuable an example of Christian marriage would be to the locals. Yet there were two questions that he would find difficult to answer: 'Who would be willing to leave the comfort of life in England for the barrenness and biting cold of the Arctic wilderness?', and 'Would it be fair to ask someone to make such a sacrifice for him?' Jack could never arrive at a final answer for either, so he did nothing about it.

The Turners were now very well known in Felixstowe. Jack and Arthur's exploits in the far north were common knowledge in the town. His mum Ellen and older brother Ted were so thankful to have him home again.

Outside the church in Felixstowe, one Sunday in November 1939, Jack was introduced to a beautiful young lady called Joan Miriam Hobart. Joan had spent much of her childhood overseas. Her father was a petroleum engineer and his work would take the family to foreign places such as Egypt. Holidays were exciting in that country. She had camped with some friends in the deserts of Egypt among the ancient ruins. She had visited the colourful street markets in Egyptian towns and had grown to love the people among whom she lived. Little did she realise that God was preparing her for work as a missionary in the Arctic regions of Canada.

The Hobart family returned to England and settled in Felixstowe in 1935, when Joan was nineteen years old. They attended the local Church of England parish church where Rev H.B. Greene continued to serve as the clergyman. While attending this church and listening to the sermons of the vicar, Joan realised that she did not know Christ Jesus personally as Saviour and Lord of her life. That changed one Sunday in 1936, when Joan fully surrendered herself to the Lord Jesus, submitting to him as King and relying on him for forgiveness and for eternal life. Her life changed and over time she felt a strong desire to serve the Lord overseas, but she didn't know where.

Jack and Joan saw much of each other during the early part of Jack's furlough. It didn't take long for a firm friendship to develop between them. They had much to talk about as both had travelled quite a lot. Jack liked Joan very much. He told her about life in the frozen wilds of the Arctic. She told him what life was like in the hot dunes of Egypt. He told her of his travelling escapades through exceptional wintry climes. She told him of her camping adventures in the hot Saharan sands. He told her of his beloved Inuit. She told him of her cherished Egyptians.

They were very happy in each other's company. They wondered if perhaps God had brought them together for a deeper purpose? Neither of them believed it was an accident. The Lord was indeed guiding the events in their lives, to bring them together that Sunday morning in the autumn of 1939.

Jack wondered if the Lord wanted Joan to share his work in the Arctic. But how could he ask this wonderful lady to join him in such a lonely, desolate and cold place, with its months of winter darkness? Surely it was too much to ask of her. He put the idea out of his mind and returned to the Arctic, arriving at Moffet Inlet on the 21st September 1940. In October that same year, Joan went back to the BCMS College in Bristol to complete her second year. Afterwards, in October 1941, she entered the East Suffolk and Ipswich Hospital to train as a nurse.

Corn Flakes, All Bran and Puffed Rice

The little radio whistled and hissed as Jack searched for an English news bulletin. Although it wasn't easy to get a good radio reception all the time in the Arctic, the device was a good link to home. Jack liked to keep up to date with news of the war. The missionaries in the Arctic felt like spectators to the conflict that raged across the world. Naturally, they worried for the safety of their loved ones.

Jack managed to get a broadcast which reported the heavy bombing of some seaside towns in England that he knew very well. He wondered how the people of Felixstowe were coping with the war. He thought of his mum and brother Ted, hoping they were managing well under the duress of enemy bombing. He remembered Joan and prayed that God would keep her safe through it all. He wondered who, if any, of his friends and neighbours back home were fighting for the Allies against Nazi Germany. Jack hated war. It was an outworking of humanity's love of darkness. A terrible business.

'A wonderful business, however, is the Lord's work in the Arctic,' Jack thought. His mind turned to the people living further west of Moffet Inlet. They were harder to reach. The people were scattered all over the place in small camps. He had some spare wood left over from the construction of the mission at Moffet Inlet. He could use it to build something small at Fort Ross, which was situated at the south-eastern end of Somerset Island, west of Baffin Island. It was an area known for its severe, ice conditions, making it a difficult place to travel. By the grace and help of God, the intrepid and zealous BCMS missionary could do it!

The Hudson's Bay Company erected a trading post at Fort Ross in 1937, the same year that Jack completed the station at Moffet Inlet. Jack knew he would meet many more Inuit looking to trade there. He could also use the new mission station as a base that would allow him to travel even further west to reach more people. As far as Jack was concerned, the Inuit were worthy of every effort and sacrifice involved to tell them about God's redeeming love.

Jack was given permission by the BCMS in London to build a new mission station at Fort Ross. The Bishop of the Arctic thought it was a great idea too. Jack had been told that a donation from a missionary colleague in the Arctic, who was to remain nameless, had been made to get the new mission station started.

Just before leaving for furlough back in England, the missionary had sold his breakfast cereals to a newly arrived worker for the Hudson's Bay Company. Cereals were a luxury food item in the Arctic and reminded Westerners of breakfast at home. The worker hadn't brought any with him and the missionary didn't need them as he was going away for six months. Arriving back in England, the money from the sale was given to the BCMS head office in London, with the express wish that it should be used to help start a mission station further west of Baffin Island in the Arctic.

So, Jack spent a number of months collecting and transporting the building materials to the area. In the Spring of 1940, the new mission house was finally ready. This is probably the only mission in the world founded on 'Corn Flakes', 'All Bran' and 'Puffed Rice', thought Jack.

Usually the Inuit are very friendly. When arriving in a camp to trade, they called on the resident missionary for hospitality. Sometimes they asked for help in understanding difficult passages of the Bible. Jack was always willing to listen and assist them as much as he could. Each evening he held a church service in the house and invited everyone in the area to come to it. It was marvellous to be able to meet the western Inuit. Yet Jack knew that he had to push out into the more treacherous terrain of their homeland if he was to reach others.

The area farther west of Moffet Inlet was renowned for even tougher travelling. It required all the skill of an experienced driver to traverse the icy fiords with a team of huskies pulling a heavily laden sledge. Jack needed all the strength that the Lord would give him to risk his life in such a climate for the spiritual good of the people.

Jack's evangelistic zeal and determination had not gone unnoticed by the Anglican Bishop of the Arctic, Archibald Lang Fleming. He was a Scottish man who had travelled in 1909 to Lake Harbour on the southern tip of Baffin Island to be a missionary. He devoted his life to the Inuit and became the first Bishop of the Arctic in 1933. He loved the Inuit and he loved the Lord. He was very keen to see the gospel of Christ proclaimed throughout the Arctic Diocese.

Fleming was a friend of the BCMS and looked after missionaries during their service there. He noticed that Jack was working very hard, so he wrote a letter to the BCMS Secretary back in London. In his communication, he said he was worried about Jack. 'Flesh and blood cannot possibly stand it very long and this causes me grave anxiety,' he wrote. Bishop Fleming knew that Jack was very proficient with the native language and was good at translating the Scriptures, the Prayer Book and hymns into Inuktitut. Perhaps Jack would give more time to that work?

It was always Jack's intention to translate as much of the Bible as he could. He wanted the local people to be able to read the Word of God in their own language. However, he still felt strongly that he must reach as many people as possible with the words of salvation.

One journey took him to King William Island, which lay about 200 miles south-west of Fort Ross. It was here that Jack and his travelling guide were met with a rather frosty reception from the locals. A small group of people, led by a young angakok, or witch doctor, met Jack as he entered the encampment.

'Who are you? What do you want?' the witch doctor asked Jack.

'My name is Jack Turner and I am known in Baffin Island as *Ayogesueye Mikeneksak*.

'Yes, I have heard of you,' said the witch doctor. 'People say that you travel across the land telling them of a man called Jesus.'

'I would like to tell you and your people about Jesus,' Jack said as he looked at the crowd. 'Can we gather together in the centre of the camp this evening?'

'We have no need of your Jesus here,' said the young man sternly.

'It's getting late,' said Jack. 'Can we set up our tents and rest here for the evening?'

The witch doctor slowly nodded in agreement.

Jack found a suitable spot at the edge of the camp and both men set to work putting up their tents. The snow was falling softly to the ground. The air was still. Jack loved evenings like this. For now, everything was calm.

As evening approached, some men from the camp returned from their hunting expeditions. Jack and his travelling companion made their way into the middle of the camp, lanterns in their hands. Jack also carried his concertina with him. They found some rocks and sat down. Jack began to play 'Jesus loves me' and the two men sang the words softly and melodically. Due to the stillness of the night, the sweet sound carried to the four corners of the village.

The people were curious and emerged from their wooden huts, tents and igloos, and followed the sound to where Jack was sitting. Even the young angakok and his wife were compelled to follow the music. The people sat down and, in the soft light of the lanterns, Jack could see many faces looking at him. When the music faded, he began to tell them of the Saviour's love for them. He spoke of the cost of that redeeming love when Jesus went to the cross in their place, for their sins. He spoke of the Spirit of Jesus who lives in his people and that evil spirits had no power over anyone who follows Christ.

The witch doctor was furious with Jack. He jumped up quickly from his seat and began to shout, pointing at Jack with every word. 'We believe that everything has a spirit, whether it's an object, a place or even a creature on the land or in the sea,' he said loudly, 'and it's my responsibility, as the angakok, to talk to those spirits on behalf of the people. I am their guide. I teach my people what they need to do to make the spirits happy. These people don't need Jesus. They need me!' he exclaimed, beating his breast with his fists.

The witch doctor grabbed his wife by the arm and pulled her up from the ground. They stomped off angrily from the small gathering. One by one, the people dispersed and made their way back to their dwellings. Jack noticed his companion speaking with an older man of the village. The conversation looked very serious.

As Jack put the concertina back in its case, his friend approached.

'You'd better be careful of that angakok,' he said. 'I have just found out something very disturbing about him.'

'Yes, so have I. It was very disturbing to see his reaction to me,' Jack said. The two men started to walk back to their tents at the edge of the encampment.

'The witch doctor's wife was married twice before. They say her first husband went mad and died by his own hand. Her second husband was killed.'

'The unfortunate girl is so young. That's really tragic news,' said Jack.

'She got the young angakok to kill her second husband!' Jack looked at his companion incredulously as both men stopped in their tracks. 'It's true, teacher. And they work their 'dark magic' together. They are determined to keep the folk believing their old pagan customs. The people are afraid of them.'

'At least now we know why they are so unfriendly,' Jack said. His heart was full of compassion for them. 'These poor souls here have a special claim to our prayers,' he said.

Jack felt that way about every Inuit he met. He would risk life and limb to bring the wonderful gospel of Christ Jesus to every person in that frozen part of the world. His reasoning was simple – the love of Christ compelled him to do so. How he longed for his Arctic neighbours to know the Saviour's love for themselves!

Going on a Bear Hunt

As the battle for freedom from Nazi tyranny continued throughout much of the world, Rev Maurice Flint became more and more restless serving at Pond Inlet. He wanted to join the Allied war effort. He wrote a letter to the BCMS in London expressing this desire. The committee understood his longing and, in 1941, Maurice left the Arctic mission to be a Chaplain in the Royal Canadian Air Force. Jack liked Maurice very much. He was a fine colleague and he served the Lord Jesus faithfully during his time in the Arctic. Jack was absolutely sure that Maurice would serve the Lord faithfully in his new role. He hoped that they would keep in touch.

That same year Jack set about his parochial[1] duties with vigour. He decided to make a trip to Igloolik, about 250 miles south of Pond Inlet, on the northern part of Melville Peninsula. He was aware that his dogs were in need of food and, as usual, Jack brought all his needs to the Lord in prayer. He knew that the area was

---

1. Relating to a church parish.

well known for deer. He was sure that the Lord would answer his prayer by providing a suitable buck or doe for food. Jack wasn't prepared for the way in which the prayer was answered.

Having spent only a few minutes in prayer, Jack could see a sledge heading towards him in the distance. As it drew closer, Jack was able to make out the face of his friend Pewatok who was holding the reins of a fine team of dogs. He was accompanied by his two young sons. The sledge was laden with walrus meat. Pewatok was known as the best hunter in the Foxe Basin area. His home was on the east side of the small islet of Jens Munk Island.

Jack had met Pewatok many times over the years. At first, the hunter didn't show much interest in the gospel of Jesus Christ. Over time he became more curious about the carpenter from Nazareth. He had even bought a New Testament that had been translated into Inuktitut. Whenever he would meet Jack, Pewatok would ask him many questions about the Bible. There were parts of it that he didn't understand, and he needed Jack to help him.

Pewatok's sledge drew up to Jack's and in a loud voice, he commanded the dogs to stop. He grinned from ear to ear as the minister approached to greet him.

'It is so good to see you and your two boys, Pewatok!' exclaimed Jack.

'Hello teacher,' said Pewatok. 'Where are you going?'

'On the way to Igloolik,' replied Jack. He turned to the boys who were sitting on top of the sledge's cargo and said, 'I have something for you both.' Jack walked back to his sledge and rummaged around in one of his bags. He pulled out two packets of sweets and gave them to the lads. Their faces lit up with glee as they held out their hands to receive the tasty gifts. Jack usually kept such treats in his travelling bag, in case he met some younger Inuit on his journeys.

'Your dogs are looking a bit scrawny, teacher,' said Pewatok.

'They are very hungry. I haven't been able to find them enough meat,' said Jack.

'Well I have just the remedy,' said Pewatok, as he patted his hand on a large bag of dissected walrus meat. 'Please take this and feed them.'

'You are very generous,' said Jack, as a sense of relief came over him. He wasn't sure if the dogs would manage to pull him to Igloolik in their present state. Although Jack was a good hunter for an outsider, he hadn't been able to find any good game recently and he was worried about his animals. Tired and hungry dogs could make any journey in the Arctic more dangerous. A stranded traveller could easily expire in the Arctic due to lack of food, harsh terrain and biting cold temperatures.

As it was early in the morning, Pewatok was disappointed that Jack couldn't stop with him for a while to talk about God. Had they met in the evening, they could have made camp for the night and spent time together reading and studying the Bible. Jack needed to get to his destination, and he couldn't afford a full day's distraction with Pewatok.

'I'm in no hurry, teacher,' said Pewatok, as he threw off his load. 'My business can wait. Can the boys and I travel with you for a while? We can make camp this evening and you can tell me more about Jesus.'

'Of course, Pewatok, that would be splendid!' exclaimed Jack. Such an answer to prayer – food for the dogs and another companion to share the journey, thought Jack.

They continued to go south and after a few hours of travel, decided to stop for the evening and build an igloo. The snow was perfect, not too powdery. It didn't take long to erect the shelter, leaving plenty of time to sit together and read the Word of God. The missionary explained the gospel of salvation to Pewatok as simply as he could. Jack longed in his heart for this man to know the Lord Jesus personally.

Early the next morning, after some further Bible study and a cup of tea, the men set off for Pewatok's camp on Jens Munk Island, at the head of Foxe Basin. They were able to reach it by way of a frozen arm of the sea. Jack had been promised plenty of dog food from there and it was on the way to Igloolik. In return for his friend's kindness, Jack promised plenty of time to read the Word of God together and answer any of Pewatok's questions.

Jack was very happy. He could think of no better travelling companion than Pewatok, especially in such an unreliable climate. The unsettled weather made the journey on to Igloolik difficult for the men and their beasts. God gave them the strength to keep going and when they arrived there, Jack spent the following days speaking to as many people as possible about the Lord Jesus. He held services and invited everyone to attend. They sang songs and Jack taught the people the gospel of Christ. This is what he did in each camp and village he visited. Every BCMS missionary in the Arctic did the same thing. Many Inuit believed in Christ and were baptised in his name. This is how God grew the church in size and number in the Arctic.

Having spent some time in Igloolik, Jack started another journey north to Fort Ross with Pewatok as his travelling companion. Once again, the food supply started to run dangerously low, for both the men and the animals. It was the time of year when the bears were coming out of their snow dens, so the men were hopeful of a good hunt. It wasn't long before they caught sight of a small bear a short distance ahead of them. It disappeared out of sight as it ran through the large ice boulders strewn across the snowy land. Pewatok gave chase, leaving Jack to catch up. By the time Jack pulled up beside his friend, he discovered that Pewatok had killed the bear and his dogs had feasted on a lot of it. The men loaded the remains of the bear onto Jack's sledge.

That morning, Jack read a promise from God in his Bible. 'And my God will supply every need of yours according to his riches in glory in Christ Jesus' (Philippians 4:19). Not only did Jack believe the promise, he claimed it for himself. He thanked God for the small bear, but he believed that it couldn't be the whole amount promised. They were in a part of the country where large bears were in abundance. 'Surely this small bear isn't 'according to his glorious riches'? thought Jack. 'It'll not last very long. It can't be the final answer to our prayers?'

It was getting dark. They would stop and make camp soon. They hadn't trekked far when suddenly Pewatok spotted a large bear beyond a barrier of rough ice. The dogs picked up the scent and veered off their track into rough ice. They got stuck. Jack and Pewatok hurriedly freed some of their best dogs from the sledges. Pewatok ran off while Jack reached for his rifle. He began to run after his companion but stopped abruptly. He couldn't leave some of the dogs behind. His dogs hadn't been fed and he was sure that they would get up to some mischief if left unattended. Jack freed the rest of his dogs. As they barked and howled in pursuit of the prey, Jack picked up his pace to follow them. Only a few moments later, some dogs turned back. Jack did his best to encourage them to run on, but it was impossible. Hungry dogs are difficult to command. He turned on his heels and headed back to the sledge. He harnessed up the dogs but didn't hitch them to the sledge. Instead he walked them a short distance from it and tethered them to a big piece of ice.

By this time, Pewatok, the dogs and the bear were a long way off. Jack was concerned that he couldn't see the way they went. He was confident that the hunter and his beasts would overtake the bear, but Jack knew that Pewatok didn't take his rifle with him. Even though his native friend was a great hunter, Jack doubted that Pewatok could kill a large polar bear with his bare hands. They are ferocious creatures, especially when cornered. He needed to help in the hunt, but which way did they go? He imagined his friend waiting in vain for his arrival.

Jack walked a short distance in the direction of the returning dogs. He stopped in front of a small hill of ice and climbed it. He listened carefully for the sounds of a hunt but couldn't hear anything except the strong wind whistling around his head. He went on a bit farther, stopped again and listened. Nothing. Not knowing which way to go, Jack knew that his only course of action was to return to the sledge. The moonlight lit up his path back to the icy hillock but then his tracks disappeared on a hard patch of snow. He kept going with his eyes to the ground, in the strong belief that he would find his tracks again. He should have been close to the sledge by now, but he didn't recognise the ice. He went in one direction and then in another but couldn't find his way.

Jack chided himself. 'How stupid can I be?' he thought. 'It's not like I haven't travelled in the Arctic before. I know the dangers. What an idiot! Heavenly Father, please help me!'

As a last resort, Jack started shouting in the hope of making the dogs howl. There was no response. He was in a very perilous position – lost, in the freezing cold Arctic, at night. He kept shouting and listening for some comeback. Then the faint sound of a voice could be heard through the wind. It was Pewatok! Jack made his way to his friend, encouraging him to keep yelling, so he could follow his voice. When Pewatok finally came into view, Jack noticed that he was near the sledge. It was too late to travel any further to Pewatok's load, so the hunter made a small igloo and the men crawled into it after giving Jack's dogs some of the bear meat from earlier.

The temperature had plummeted to minus 34 degrees Celsius. It wasn't much warmer inside the snow house. They had no light and no fire, so they munched on frozen bear meat and biscuits before lying down. But they were too cold to sleep much. With no proper warm meal in their bellies, the men felt the cold badly when they started their onward journey early the next morning.

Unreliable weather slowed everything down. The upside for Pewatok was more time to read the Bible with the missionary and have his questions answered. Both men were feeding mightily on every word that came from the mouth of the Lord. However, there was hardly any bear meat left with which the men or dogs could satisfy their physical hunger. Jack held on to the promise from God's Word, that the Lord would supply all their needs. And sure enough, two days later, just after midnight, Pewatok popped his head in the doorway of Jack's igloo and announced that the dogs had been fed. He had tracked a large female bear that day and was successful in the hunt.

'Praise God!' exclaimed Jack. 'God is the giver of every good and perfect gift,' he said. Both men gave thanks to the Lord who had answered their prayers, fulfilled his promise and abundantly met their needs.

There was another prayer that Jack wanted God to answer abundantly. He prayed that many Inuit people would hear the gospel of Christ, repent and believe. He prayed that especially for his friend Pewatok. He wanted Pewatok to know the love of Christ in his own life. He begged God to open the eyes of his companion, that he might see King Jesus, turn to him and live. Wonderfully, God answered this prayer too. On Sunday, 25th January 1942, Pewatok was baptised by Canon Jack Turner at Moffet Inlet, as a public declaration of his faith in Christ. Hallelujah!

Here comes the Bride

With the departure of Rev Maurice Flint from Pond Inlet, Jack was left on his own for two years to care for the Inuit in his territory. He set about the usual task of travelling to visit his parish during this time and managed an astounding four thousand miles by dog sledge and foot. It was a remarkable feat of endurance by anyone's standards. During those moments of good travelling he would think of Joan. She was willing to follow God's call and serve the Lord anywhere. Before Jack's departure from Felixstowe, they wondered together if that place would be the Arctic. As there was no clear guidance about that, they went their separate ways, promising to keep in touch by telegram and letter.

Rev Tom Daulby joined Jack in 1942 and stayed at Pond Inlet. This enabled Jack to move back to the mission house at Moffet Inlet. His thoughts turned once again to Miss Hobart. Before, he had thought the sacrifice for Joan was too much to bear. But recently he had been thinking about it in a different way. He wondered if it was right to take upon himself the whole responsibility of deciding whether she should join him in that uninviting land or not. Certainly, God had caused them to be in Felixstowe at the same time. These things do not happen by coincidence. Perhaps it was the Lord's way of making known to Joan the mission field in which he wanted her to serve him? If so, God's purpose shouldn't be hindered any longer. Therefore, Jack asked her to join him in the Arctic the following year. He wrote a letter to Joan which reached her on Thursday, 11th November 1943.

By this time, Joan had completed two years of her nursing training. She was convinced that the time was right to join Canon Turner in the Arctic, so she wrote to Dr Bartlett for guidance.

Sunday, 14th November 1943
Dear Dr Bartlett,
On Thursday evening (11th November) I received a letter from Canon J.H. Turner in which he asked me to join him in the Arctic next year. I trust he has corresponded with you on this subject as I would be most grateful if you would put it before the BCMS Committee at their next meeting.

The Lord's will is now very clear to us both. We have both had a long period in which to think it over and there is no doubt in our minds as to it being to the furtherance of the Lord's Kingdom.

Many thanks for all the support you will give us in this matter, because of your opinion of Jack Turner.

Yours very sincerely,

Joan Hobart

Jack had written a letter to Dr Bartlett dated 13th August, 1943. In it he described the work of the gospel of Christ among the Inuit and his desire to remain at Moffet Inlet to do some more translation. Dr Bartlett received the letter on 10th November, 1943:

13th August 1943 (received 10th November 1943)

Dear Dr Bartlett,

Thank you for sending Tom Daulby. His coming is a great help. He is now holding the fort at Pond Inlet. He has been able to do some travelling, is making good progress with the language and is settling down to life very well. We are still able to report a keenness on the part of the Inuit to hear our message and the great interest in the study of the Scriptures continues. The Bible is certainly reverenced and many of the Inuit, if not most, seem anxious to follow its teaching. Nevertheless, the temptations are great, and they need much prayer if they are to be led into the liberty of the sons of God. We too need your prayers that we may always represent our Lord aright.

With affectionate regards, as always.

Yours very sincerely,

Jack Turner

P.S. If it is possible to send Miss Hobart next year, I should be glad to remain here an extra year. That is, until she has been in the field at least two years. By that time – if the Lord will – I should have been able to get a great amount of this work on the Inuit Old Testament and Prayer Book completed. I commit these matters to your earnest consideration. I know they will have that careful thought you have always shown with regard to all our affairs. I trust you can feel that same confidence in us that we always have in you. If you have not seen fit to meet all our requests, I know it is because you have felt good reason for the line you took, and God's glory has always been your motive.   *JHT*

Dr Bartlett replied to Joan only a few days after receiving her letter in November and he was able to respond regarding Jack's request for her to join him.

Wednesday, 17th November 1943
Dear Miss Hobart,
Yes, I have received a letter from Canon Turner. I am bringing your letter before the BCMS Committee on the 30th November, after which I will write to you again.

Meanwhile, you will be wise to gain as much experience as you can in midwifery, for practical knowledge of that section of nursing will be valuable.

I am very sincerely yours,
Dr Bartlett

In the following summer of 1944, Dr Bartlett wrote to Jack and sent it by airmail:

Saturday, 17th June 1944
My dear Turner,
I expect your thoughts, and certainly our thoughts have been much upon the possibility of getting Miss Hobart out to you this summer. The difficulties are enormous and the uncertainties many. Nevertheless, we pray that she may duly arrive and that you will be united, I presume at Pond Inlet, by Mr Daulby this summer. Anything that we could do has not been left undone to realise this, and at our BCMS Annual Meeting on 1st May 1944, Miss Hobart gave a public testimony to the reality of her conversion to Christ and to her wish to devote her life with you in the furtherance of God's work among the Inuit. It was a grand meeting, the best we have held during war time. Thus, she became personally known to many BCMS members and their and our wishes for God's blessing upon your union accompany Joan and will be delivered by her to you when your marriage takes place.

Our love in the Lord.
Yours most sincerely,
Dr Bartlett

In June 1944, Miss Hobart and her friend, Miss Jean Greenlaw, who would be her bridesmaid, started the long and perilous wartime journey to the Polar North on board the *SS Nascopie*. This was the same ship that took Jack to his most northerly parish on Baffin Island back in 1929. On this journey, the ship didn't creak or moan as it navigated the waters of Hudson's Bay because Joan was arriving at the time of year when the Arctic was thawed out. The weathered coastline looked resplendent in the early morning light.

In her daily diary, Joan described the arrival of the boat to Pond Inlet on Tuesday, 29th August 1944, her special day:

By 3 am we had dropped anchor, so I dressed and went out on to the deck. The beauty of the morning and of the scenery was indescribable. The sun was just rising over the snow-capped mountains at the back of the Post. The air was frosty and invigorating and the deep blue sea was unruffled by any wind. This glorious morning was a forerunner of a wonderfully sunny day which proved to be the warmest and most perfect of the whole summer. It wasn't long before Jack had come on board and we met again after just over four years. It was the Lord's doing and marvellous in our eyes.

Immediately they went ashore where Jack introduced his beloved to Tom. 'Joan, I would like you to meet Tom Daulby,' he said.

'Very pleased to meet you Mr Daulby,' said Joan as she held out her hand.

Tom shook it enthusiastically. 'I am very pleased to meet you too Miss Hobart,' said Tom. 'Jack hasn't told me very much about you, being a private man himself, but I look forward to getting to know you over time.'

Joan smiled. She knew that Jack wasn't the sort of man who would gush about his new bride, but he did love her with all his heart. Jack knew Miss Hobart would be a wonderful partner to share his life, and to share in the Lord's work in the Polar North.

'This is Miss Jean Greenlaw,' Joan said to Tom. 'Jean is my bridesmaid.'

'Lovely to meet you Miss Greenlaw. It's a long way to come just for a wedding,' Tom said curiously.

'Oh, I'm not just here for the wedding,' laughed Jean. 'I'm a nurse, like Joan. I will be moving down to the hospital at Pangnirtung in a few days.'

'Where Arthur is?' asked Tom.

'Yes,' smiled Jean. 'Where Arthur is.'

The wedding was to begin at 10 am at the mission house, so the introductions were kept brief. There would be time to chat more during the reception after the marriage ceremony.

The ladies went up to the mission house to get dressed, accompanied by some of the male passengers who kindly carried their suitcases for them. The wedding cake was in a large cardboard box and needed careful transportation from the boat to the house. It was placed on a small sledge and carefully pushed to the front door.

With the help of some local Inuit, Jack and Tom had spent the previous day getting the wedding venue ready for the big occasion. The folding doors between the kitchen and dining room were thrown open. Chairs were placed along one side of the room. They were occupied by locals who came to witness the special event. A very narrow aisle was left for the bride, who was escorted by a friend of Jack's, Mr Anderson of the Hudson's Bay Company at Ungava. So, the aisle was from one end of the room, past the warm stove, to a table that was placed under the window in the centre of the end wall!

At the table stood Rev Daulby, the bridegroom, the bridesmaid, and the best man called Hugh Longfield. Mr Longfield was working at the meteorological station located in Arctic Bay. Jack spent many days in Arctic Bay, meeting the local hunters who stopped there to trade at the HBC trading post and sharing the gospel of Christ with them. Over time, he struck up a good friendship with Hugh, and it seemed good to ask him to be his best man.

As Joan walked down the aisle, linking Mr Anderson's arm with hers, she noticed two Royal Canadian Mounted Police Officers standing with the wedding party at the table. *Well, the house is so full, where else could they be!* she chuckled to herself.

When the ceremony and signing of the register book were over, the room transformed into a reception room, with food and drink for all to share. It was a great celebration and the beginning of a wonderful partnership.

Bishop Fleming had recommended the newly-weds stay at Pond Inlet for the year, to allow Joan time to adjust to her new surroundings. In his opinion, Moffet Inlet was too isolated and too scarcely populated for Mrs Turner to begin her new life and ministry with Jack. Staying at Pond Inlet gave her time to learn the language. It also allowed her to get accustomed to Jack's prolonged absences from the mission house as he went about his pastoral visitations across his parish, without feeling too lonely.

The following summer of 1945 saw two momentous occasions in the life of the Turner household: the birth of a daughter and a relocation of family life. On Monday, 4th June at 10.15 am, June Mary was born. Both Jack and Joan saw her as a blessing from the Lord. The locals adored her. Sadly for them, the Turners moved to Moffet Inlet shortly after June's birth. They wouldn't get the chance to see her grow up in their midst. But they all understood why the Turners needed to move. From Moffet Inlet, Jack had more opportunity to meet the folks who lived and hunted in the western parts of the Arctic. They needed to hear the gospel of Christ too. Jack was also able to give more uninterrupted time to his translation work. There was much he wanted to do. He was so thankful to God for the provision of a good and godly wife to share the work. She attended to the medical needs of the locals who came to the mission house for help. When Jack was away, she led the services. Jack saw his wife as a true partner and blessing from the Lord.

The following September, Barbara Grace, their second daughter, was born at Moffet Inlet – another beautiful, healthy daughter for them to love and nurture. The Turners were enjoying life to the full. They found great satisfaction serving the Inuit day by day. They cared for each other and loved each other deeply. They never felt lonely or isolated. They had the assurance that they were working with their Lord and Saviour. They knew that they were in the place that God wanted them to be.

The Turners were very content.

Operation Canon

John Cormack arrived in Moffet Inlet four days after Jack's accident occurred. He was the man in charge of the Hudson's Bay Company trading post at Arctic Bay. When he learned of Jack's misfortune from David Tongalok, he decided to make the journey south to Pond Inlet, to see if he could be of any assistance to the Turner family. He brought with him two Inuit men. Mrs Turner needed all the help she could get, and he knew that a rescue would be attempted by the authorities in Canada.

The small group of men entered the mission house to see how Jack was. He had regained consciousness and Joan was using all her skill as a nurse to look after him as best she could.

'How is he today, Mrs Turner?' asked Mr Cormack, as he entered through the front door of the mission house.

'He is awake and talking,' Joan answered, 'but he's in a lot of pain. He also hurt his back when he fell down the steps.'

Jack heard Mr Cormack's voice, and asked him to come closer to where he was lying on the floor.

'John, it is so good to see you,' said Jack.

'How are you feeling Canon Turner?' asked Mr Cormack, kneeling beside his bed.

'I am doing okay, John. I have the most wonderful nurse looking after me.' Mrs Turner smiled. 'I do apologise that I cannot welcome you properly into our home, John. I am so sorry for all the trouble I am causing you.'

'Canon Turner, think nothing of it. You are not causing me any trouble at all. It is my pleasure to be of assistance to you and Mrs Turner. I have brought some men with me. We shall do everything in our power to help get you to a hospital. Then you can get better and come back to us.'

Jack was grateful for Mr Cormack's willingness to help in his time of need. He thanked God for such good friends.

A while back, Jack had built a storehouse out the back of the mission station. In the summer the family used it as a little summer cottage. It was well insulated and comfortable. Mr Cormack and his men, accompanied by David Tongalok and his two sons, started to clear it in preparation for any who might respond to the radio appeal. They put in a stove, some beds, tables and chairs and a basin for washing. When it was ready, all they could do was wait.

The Department of National Defence, the Army and Royal Canadian Air Force organised a rescue team of four paratroopers and a flight crew for a Dakota aeroplane. The only way into Moffet Inlet quickly was to drop the rescuers by parachute from the plane into the area. However, Moffet Inlet was unchartered territory and, without maps, it would be impossible. Then Colonel Graham Rowley remembered that he met Canon Turner and Rev Flint whilst on an Arctic Expedition with the British and Canadian forces. He knew that Flint had experience of Moffet Inlet too and was now serving as a Chaplain in the Canadian Air Force. He picked up the telephone and asked Maurice if he could help.

That previous summer, Maurice had decided to get rid of Arctic papers and photographs that he didn't need anymore. He had taken a bundle of the papers and thrown them onto the fire that was burning brightly in his sitting room. As they had begun to burn, he had noticed some old sketch maps of the Northern Territories and he had pulled them quickly from the fire. He thought that they may be useful one day! When he received the call from Colonel Rowley, he had all the maps and photos that the team needed for their rescue.

Maurice boarded the overnight train to Ottawa. The next morning, he went to a conference of Army and Air Force officials. When they listened to what Maurice had to say about getting to Moffet Inlet, they decided a rescue was possible. Then Rev Flint was sent by plane to Western Canada to meet the rescue team. He arrived at his location by midnight and was immediately led to a large room filled with people who were waiting on him to arrive. This was the headquarters of 'Operation Canon'. There was no time to sleep. He was asked to brief the rescue team about travelling to Moffet Inlet. They needed to know everything he could tell them about the landscape, the people, the climate and what clothes to wear to stay warm. The soldiers asked questions all through the night.

Early the next morning, on Thursday, 2nd October 1947, the Dakota aircraft was ready to fly. It was loaded with equipment, food and medical supplies and a very heavy radio set. Once the paratroopers and aircrew were on board, it thundered down the runway gaining speed until it finally took flight. The heavily-laden plane climbed doggedly into the overcast clouds of that cold October morning and out of sight. It's 1,700 mile journey had begun. It was going to be a difficult rescue.

Moffet Inlet is situated north of the magnetic North Pole, so their magnetic compasses were useless. The lakes and rivers were frozen and covered with snow. All of these things meant that the crew would not be able to pinpoint a location. Although the maps that Maurice had drawn during his time as a missionary there were helpful, they were not drawn to scale.

The mission was built on a small piece of land that jutted out into the Inlet. It was also at the base of a 600 foot cliff. It was surrounded by frozen saltwater. These conditions made it too dangerous to drop the soldiers and any supplies that were needed at the house. A safer dropping area would be found a few miles further inland. If only they could find the Turners' house.

Mrs Turner woke at 6 am on Saturday, 4th October 1947. She looked out of her bedroom window and saw nothing but fog. Her heart sank. A plane would not be able to find them in such atrocious weather conditions. About noon, as she was sitting with Jack, holding his hand and praying, she heard the sweet sound of roaring engines pass overhead. It had missed them. She felt herself asking those awful questions, would it return? Would they be able to see the house? Would they be in time to help her husband?

Quite suddenly the sky cleared and there was a hole in the fog around the mission. The plane had circled, and the aircrew could see the house through the gap in the clouds. The Dakota swooped lower and dropped a note with some metal panels which landed near the house. It was retrieved by one of the local men who brought it swiftly to Mrs Turner. She read it carefully:

We are here to help Canon Turner. It is proposed to parachute a small party including a medical officer for this purpose. Owing to the ruggedness of the ground, men cannot be dropped safely near the mission but we intend dropping less fragile stores at the mission and the men and other equipment in the deer country. Divide your Inuit into two parties. Keep one party at the mission and send the other to the top of the cliffs to go to the aid of the party when they drop. Please acknowledge by signalling a reply to this question with the panels attached. Are we still in time to be of help?

If the answer was 'yes', then Joan needed to put one panel on the ground. If 'no', then two panels. Without a doubt the answer was 'yes'. Joan gave instruction to the bearer of the note, to place one panel on the ground beside the house.

In the meantime, the aircrew surveyed the surrounding country for a good dropping area for the paratroopers and supplies. When they flew back over the mission, they saw the single panel lying on the ground. They were in time to help.

The paratroopers buckled on their harnesses and strapped on their steel helmets. As the Dakota approached a frozen lake six miles further inland from the Moffet Inlet house, the men and their supplies fell from the skies. The four-man crew was led by Captain Guy d'Artois. It included a medical officer called Captain Ross Willoughby, and Signals Sergeants W.W. Judd and A.R. Cook. Along with the aircrew, they were a brave group who had proved themselves in the lines of battle as capable, resourceful and ready to face any difficulty. This rescue mission would require all of their skills.

On the ground, Sergeant Judd sent a radio message back to the captain of the Dakota that all had landed safely. Captain d'Artois started to trek over land towards the mission house and was eventually met by one of the Inuit men who was to act as his guide.

The other three soldiers headed for the coast and were picked up by a boat that had been sent from the Turners' home.

The weather was so unsettled, it took two days for the group to meet up again at Moffet Inlet. Once there, Captain Willoughby's first job was to evaluate Canon Turner's condition. He could tell straight away that Jack was paralysed down the left side of his body. He noticed a large bedsore at the base of his back that would need a clean bandage every day.

The team settled into the small storehouse and assessed the situation over the following two days. They determined that if Jack was able to be moved and if the weather settled down, then perhaps they should move Jack to somewhere less remote. It would make his extraction from the Arctic to the hospital in Winnipeg a bit easier. Mr Cormack suggested, and Captain Willoughby agreed, that a move to Arctic Bay seventy miles north would be good for Jack. There were better facilities there. It was easier for a plane to land there too and there was a good radio at the HBC's trading post. As the team leader, Captain d'Artois decided they should try to move Canon Turner the following day.

The weather was so inclement that it delayed departure until Tuesday, 9th October. The motorboats at the mission house were loaded with supplies for the journey. They made a stretcher for Jack out of some wood and stretched a couple of skins over the frame. Then they carried the seriously ill missionary to old

Ebenezer. The path from the house was so icy and rough with rocks, the men slipped and stumbled their way to the boat. They tried as hard as they could to get the Canon's boat out of the bay, but it was impossible. They had to turn back to the house and try again the next day. This attempt was also thwarted by bad ice conditions and engine failure. Jack was out in the cold for too long, so they abandoned that voyage and returned to the mission house. Everyone was bitterly disappointed. At no point did Jack utter a word of complaint. The soldiers then realised the mettle of the man who served God in those northerly climes. But it was clear to them that a closer extraction point needed to be found.

Thousands of people throughout Canada were upholding the Turners in prayer and they were eagerly waiting for news. Reports were silent though, as the long-range radio that the soldiers had brought with them had broken when it was dropped from the plane. The Signal Sergeants spent days trying to repair it and eventually got it working on Saturday, 18th October. They were able to connect with outside radio stations and give updates concerning Operation Canon. However, the climate in the Arctic at that time of year made it impossible to get Jack out of Moffet Inlet.

During those days of waiting, the Inuit called at the house or wrote the Canon letters. Where necessary, he wrote back, using Rebecca as his secretary. Sunday services continued in the kitchen. The study door was kept open so Jack could join in.

Meanwhile Captain d'Artois set about the tough task of finding a closer landing site for the plane. On each excursion he always had a local person with him as a guide. Sometimes he walked on the land. Sometimes he used the boat. Later he travelled by dog team and sledge. On one occasion he fell through the ice but was pulled to safety by his travelling companion. It wasn't until November that the brave captain found just the right landing strip for the Dakota. For eleven days he camped at a lake twenty-three miles south of Moffet Inlet. It had frozen enough to withstand the weight of a Dakota aircraft landing on it. During this time, he was caught in a severe blizzard. The snowstorm blew vigorously and prevented an Inuit reaching him with fuel for his stove and lamp. The captain was forced to live for a couple of days without heat or light. The strong winds smashed the tent pole and he had no choice but to remain in his sleeping bag until the storm blew over. Never before had he felt so cold and alone.

He returned to the mission on Thursday, 13th November. Captain d'Artois ordered his men and the other occupants of the house to prepare for the journey south to the lake.

On the day the evacuation was to take place, the Inuit came to say goodbye to their beloved teacher, known throughout the land as 'Mikeneksak'. Jack said his last prayers with them. They stood around his bed with their heads bowed. Tears filled their eyes, as they committed each other to God's keeping. Pewatok was there. He accompanied Jack on many dangerous journeys throughout the Arctic during the Canon's missionary service. Now he would drive his dear friend on his last sledge journey to the waiting plane.

The plane landed safely on the frozen lake on Friday, 21st November 1947. Canon and Mrs Turner, their two daughters, Rebecca and the rescue team boarded *The Blizzard Belle*, the name given to the aircraft, and were flown southwards to Winnipeg.

The plane touched down the following afternoon. A crowd of officials, press photographers, friends and well-wishers had gathered at the airport to welcome them. Mrs Turner and the girls were taken to the home of a generous and kind lady called Mrs Folliott, who lovingly cared for them during their time in Winnipeg. Her home wasn't too far away from the Winnipeg General Hospital where Jack was being treated by a team of specialists. It was easy for them to visit Jack every day. But his condition was so serious that on the morning of Tuesday, 9th December 1947, Jack went to be with his Lord. That afternoon, Bishop Fleming sent a cablegram to the BCMS General Secretary:

Rev A T Houghton, with profound sorrow we advise you Canon Turner died this morning. On your behalf we will look after his family and affairs. Please advise the Canon's family.

Mrs Turner and her two daughters travelled back to England shortly after Jack's death. Joan wanted her third child to be born in England. She was so sad that Jack didn't live to see the birth of another beautiful daughter whom she called Faith. She was born on Monday, 22nd December 1947.

* * *

From the day that John became a devoted servant of Christ, he was a new creature. He had one aim and one object in life – to glorify God and to serve him to the limit of his capacity.

In his eighteen years as a BCMS missionary, Jack travelled nearly 25,000 miles by dog team and sledge to bring the gospel of Jesus Christ to lost souls in the Polar North. Many wintry journeys were fraught with danger. It didn't deter him, for the love of Christ compelled him to do it. He loved the Inuit because of the strength of the loyalty and devotion he had to Jesus Christ as Saviour, Lord and King. However, Jack's real achievement was seen in the transformed lives of the men and women, boys and girls whom he had led to the Lord Jesus Christ. John Hudspith Turner fought the good fight, he finished the race and he kept the faith (2 Timothy 4:7).

The task in the Canadian Arctic, however, is not finished. The cry of the gospel of Jesus Christ still goes out: *For 'everyone who calls on the name of the Lord will be saved.' And how are they to believe in him of whom they have never heard? And how are they to hear without someone preaching? And how are they to preach unless they are sent? As it is written, 'How beautiful are the feet of those who preach the good news!'* (Romans 10:13-15).

Author Information

The story of the Church's mission to the Inuit in the cold and demanding climate of the Arctic, is one that is filled with sacrifice and great achievements. Canon Turner was a BCMS missionary for eighteen years in the Arctic. During that time, he endeavoured, at great personal risk, to seek out the spiritually lost in the icy wilds and perpetual darkness of many an Arctic winter. Why? Because of the love of God and the testimony of Jesus Christ (Revelation 1:9).

Today more than ever, we need to be reminded, encouraged and challenged by the tremendous example of people such as Jack Turner, who gave up the comforts and opportunities of life in England to tell the Arctic people of Christ and his love for them.

David Luckman comes from Northern Ireland. He is a graduate of Oak Hill College and King's College, London. He taught Religious Education in a secondary school in England, before being ordained as a Church of Ireland minister. For a number of years, he was the Ireland Director of Crosslinks. It was during this time that he came across Jack Turner and the story of the BCMS mission to the Arctic. He felt that Jack Turner's story was definitely worth telling.

David is married and has two daughters.

Jack Turner
Timeline

1905 John Hudspith Turner born on 14th July.
His father, Thomas Turner, dies in April.

1914 Great War begins in Europe on 28th July.

1918 Great War ends on 11th November.

1921 Jack begins training as a chemist in Ipswich.

1922 The Bible Churchmen's Missionary Society is formed on 27th October.

1925 Jack comes to saving faith in Jesus Christ at one of Reginald T. Nash's meetings on 20th December.

1926 Jack Turner offered a place at the BCMS Training College for Men on 7th April.
Bishop Stringer of Canada visits the college appealing for missionaries to go to the Arctic with the gospel of Christ.

1929 Jack finishes training at the BCMS College. He travels to Quebec in Canada, where he is ordained for ministry on 12th July.

1933 Jack arrives back in England on furlough.

1934 Jack returns to the Arctic in July.

1937 George VI's coronation at Westminster Abbey, London.

1938 Jack is awarded the King George VI Coronation Medal for 'Arctic Service' in September.

1939 Jack is made Canon of the Cathedral of All Saints, Aklavik in the Diocese of the Arctic.

The Second World War starts in Europe on 3rd September.

Jack returns to England for his second furlough on 28th October.

Jack meets Miss Joan Hobart for the first time, in November.

1940 Jack sets sail for the Arctic on 24th June.

Jack starts to build the mission station at Fort Ross.

1944 Canon Turner marries Miss Joan Hobart at Pond Inlet on 29th August.

1945 June Mary Turner is born on 4th June at Moffet Inlet.

Second World War ends in September.

1946 Barbara Grace Turner is born on 21st September at Moffet Inlet.

1947 Jack's accident happens at Moffet Inlet on 24th September.

Operation Canon starts in October.

Jack dies from his injuries on 9th December at Winnipeg General Hospital.

Joan, June and Barbara return to England on 17th December.

Faith Turner born on 22nd December in England.

Thinking Further Topics

1. 24th September, 1947

The Bible Churchmen's Missionary Society adopted
Revelation 1:9 as a motto, 'for the word of God and
the testimony of Jesus Christ'. The spread of the
gospel of Christ was the main reason any missionary
venture was undertaken. Is this a good enough reason
for you to get involved in God's mission to the world?
Do you tell your friends about God's love for them?
If not, why not?

2. Fun and Adventure

The Turners lived in a small house, but they were very
happy. Do you think you would be happy living in a big
house or a small house? Is it important to have many
nice things? Read Luke 18 – rich people are not always
happy people. Read Luke 19. What made Zacchaeus
full of joy?

3. A Change of Direction

Many people think that they will get into heaven
just by doing good things. Do you like to do good
things? Do you think that you will get into heaven
just by doing good things? Read Ephesians 2:8-9 and
Isaiah 64:6. Jack heard that Jesus Christ died on the
cross in his place and for his sins. If we can get into
heaven by doing good deeds, why do you think Jesus

would die on a cross for us? Read Romans 5:8 and Ephesians 2:1-10.

4. Preparation for Service

Before Jack became a disciple of Christ, he was bored at church. Are you ever bored at church? Do you think it is important to hear the Word of God preached each week at church? What should be the outcome of hearing God's Word and putting what you hear into practice in your life? Read Colossians 1:9-12.

5. Journey to the Arctic

Jack thanked the Lord every day for the many blessings that He brought into his life. Do you think it important to say 'thank you' to God? Why, or why not? Do you regularly thank God for anything He has blessed you with? Read Psalm 95.

6. A Missionary's Life

Jack Turner and Harold Duncan were both musical and used their talents to lead the Inuit in singing praise to God. Do you have any talents that you can use to bring glory to God? It doesn't have to be music; it can be anything. If you are not sure, ask someone who knows you really well and perhaps they can help you identify what gifts and talents you have. Read Romans 12:4-8.

7. On the Trail

Often on the trail, Jack faced situations that might cause despair. The blizzards stopped Jack travelling at times. The difficult landscape and frozen saltwater often damaged his sledge. Sometimes he couldn't get enough food to feed his dogs. When you feel that things are difficult in your life, what do you do to get through them? Do you call upon the Lord for help and strength? Read Psalm 132.

8. Returning Home

When Jack went back to England, he visited churches to remind them how much God loves them. He also told people how much God loves the Inuit. He described the work he was doing in the Arctic, all because of the deep conviction that people need to hear the good news of Jesus and be saved. There are many people in the world today who still need to hear the good news of Jesus. Have you ever wondered what you can do about it? Jesus promises to be with us whatever we do for Him. Read Matthew 28:16-20

9. A New Mission Station

The Inuit of the Arctic speak a language called Inuktitut. Jack and the other missionaries in that land had to learn the language so that they could talk with the local people. It also meant that Jack could spend time translating the Bible into Inuktitut so people could read it for themselves. Do you think it is important for people to have the Bible in their own language? Do you think it is important to read the Bible every day? Why? Read Matthew 4:4, Luke 21:33 and Psalm 119.

10. Corn Flakes, All Bran and Puffed Rice

As Jack pushed further into the Western regions of the Arctic from the mission station at Fort Ross, he met lots of people who didn't believe the same things he did about God and creation. Was Jack right to try and change their minds? Does it really matter what people believe about God? Read John 14:6 and Philippians 2:1-2.

11. Going on a Bear Hunt

Every time Jack met Pewatok, he told him about Jesus Christ. He did it often and simply. He answered Pewatok's questions from the Bible as clearly and helpfully as he could. Pewatok's greatest need was to have his sins forgiven by Jesus – indeed, our greatest need is to have our sins forgiven by Jesus. Do you think this is our greatest need or is there a greater need that you can think of? Read Mark 2:1-12.

12. Here come the Bride

Jack's missionary service in the Arctic was noticed and rewarded by those in high office in Government and the Diocese of the Arctic. What reward do you think Christians should seek for their service of Jesus

Christ? Read 1 Corinthians 9:25, 2 Timothy 4:7-8, and James 1:12.

13. Operation Canon

The rescue team of Operation Canon risked their lives to help Jack and his family in their hour of need. What lengths would you go to in order to help someone who needed it? Read John 15:9-17 and read Philippians 2:5-11 to see the lengths that Jesus goes to in order to help us!

Jack Turner served the Lord with gladness for many years in the Arctic. When the time came, he was not afraid to die. Why do you think he had no fear of death? Are you afraid of it? If you love Jesus and follow him, there is no need to fear. Read Romans 6:23, Isaiah 25:6-9, 1 Corinthians 15:55-56 and John 11:25-25.

Members of the OPERATION CANON Rescue Team

Captain Lionel Guy d'Artois, D.S.O. of Rivers, Manitoba and Montreal, commander of the paratroop expedition.

Captain Ross W. Willoughby, R.C.A.M.C., of Rivers, Manitoba and Toronto, paratroop medical officer.

Sergeant Howard C. Cook, of Calgary, wireless operator.

Sergeant W.W. Judd, of Port Arthur, wireless operator.

Flying Officer Robert Carson Race of Hilliers, British Columbia, and Winnipeg, pilot of the Dakota aircraft, *The Blizzard Belle*.

Flying Officer K.O. Moore, D.S.O., of Vancouver, co-pilot.

Flying Officer Clifford C. McMillan, of Saskatoon and Winnipeg, navigator.

Flight Lieutenant Anthony B. Morabito, D.F.C. of New Westminster, British Columbia, wireless operator.

Sergeant K.C. Swinford, of Toronto, crewman.

Corporal L.D. Hawkins, of Winnipeg, crewman.

Corporal James Paterson Rae, R.C.A.F., of Cupar, Saskatchewan, crewman.

Medical Specialists at Winnipeg General Hospital

Rev Dr Glover, co-operator in the care of Canon Turner.

Dr H.M. Speechly, co-ordinator in the care of Canon Turner.

Dr Oliver Waugh, surgeon on injuries to the brain and skull.

Dr E.J. Washington, Eye, Ear and Nose specialist.

Dr Gilbert Adamson, neurologist.

Dr Arthur Childe, radiologist.

Burial Site

John Hudspith Turner is buried in the cemetery of St. John's Cathedral Churchyard in Winnipeg, Manitoba, Canada.

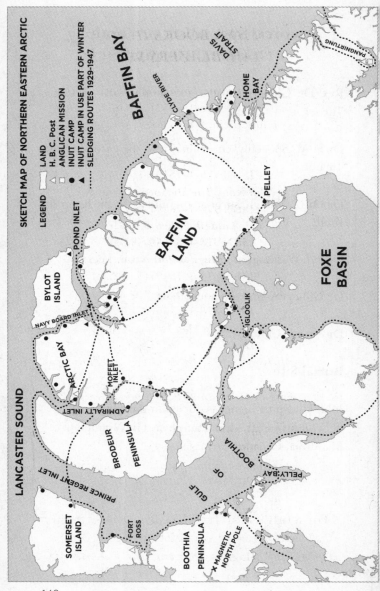

SKETCH MAP OF NORTHERN EASTERN ARCTIC

LEGEND
LAND
H. B. C. Post
ANGLICAN MISSION
INUIT CAMP
INUIT CAMP IN USE PART OF WINTER
SLEDGING ROUTES 1929-1947

BAFFIN BAY

DAVIS STRAIT

PANGNIRTUNG

HOME BAY

CLYDE RIVER

PELLEY

BAFFIN LAND

FOXE BASIN

POND INLET

BYLOT ISLAND

NAVY BOARD INLET

IGLOOLIK

ARCTIC BAY

MOFFET INLET

ADMIRALTY INLET

BRODEUR PENINSULA

LANCASTER SOUND

PRINCE REGENT INLET

SOMERSET ISLAND

FORT ROSS

BOOTHIA PENINSULA

GULF OF BOOTHIA

PELLY BAY

x MAGNETIC NORTH POLE

OTHER BOOKS IN THE
TRAIL BLAZERS SERIES

Augustine, The Truth Seeker
ISBN 978-1-78191-296-6
John Calvin, After Darkness Light
ISBN 978-1-78191-550-9
Fanny Crosby, The Blind Girl's Song
ISBN 978-1-78191-163-1
John Knox, The Sharpened Sword
ISBN 978-1-78191-057-3
Eric Liddell, Finish the Race
ISBN 978-1-84550-590-5
Martin Luther, Reformation Fire
ISBN 978-1-78191-521-9
Robert Moffat, Africa's Brave Heart
ISBN 978-1-84550-715-2
D.L. Moody, One Devoted Man
ISBN 978-1-78191-676-6
Mary of Orange, At the Mercy of Kings
ISBN 978-1-84550-818-0
Patrick of Ireland: The Boy who Forgave
ISBN: 978-1-78191-677-3
John Stott, The Humble Leader
ISBN 978-1-84550-787-9
Ulrich Zwingli, Shepherd Warrior
ISBN 978-1-78191-803-6

For a full list of Trail Blazers, please see our
website: www.christianfocus.com
All Trail Blazers are available as e-books

TRAIL BLAZERS

• Thomas Clarkson •

THE GIANT WITH ONE IDEA

Emily J. Maurits

Thomas Clarkson
The Giant With One Idea
Emily J. Maurits

- Biography for 9- 4s
- British abolitionist
- Part of the successful Trail Blazers series

Thomas Clarkson was the son of a clergyman who lived in a time when it was legal to buy and sell slaves. He believed this was wrong, and campaigned to make sure this changed. He was instrumental in making sure that no human being could be bought or sold in the British Empire.

ISBN: 978-1-5271-0677-2

CHRISTIAN FOCUS PUBLICATIONS

Christian Focus / Christian Heritage / CF4K / Mentor

Christian Focus Publications publishes books for adults and children under its four main imprints: Christian Focus, CF4K, Mentor and Christian Heritage. Our books reflect our conviction that God's Word is reliable and Jesus is the way to know him, and live for ever with him.

Our children's publication list covers pre-school to early teens. We also publish personal and family devotional titles, biographies and inspirational stories that children will love.

From pre-school board books to teenage apologetics, we have it covered!

Christian Focus Publications Ltd,
Geanies House, Fearn, Ross-shire,
IV20 1TW, Scotland,
United Kingdom.
www.christianfocus.com

Find us at our web page:
www.christianfocus.com

CF4·K
Because you're never
too young to know Jesus